STRANGERS IN THE GARDEN

STRANGERS IN THE GARDEN
The Secret Lives of Our Favorite Flowers

 ANDREW SMITH

M&S

A PageWave book
published by McClelland & Stewart Ltd.

National Library of Canada Cataloguing in Publication

Smith, Andrew, 1947-
Strangers in the garden : the secret lives of our favorite flowers /
Andrew Smith.

"A PageWave Book".
Includes bibliographical references and index.
ISBN 0-7710-8098-0

1. Flowers--History. 2. Plant introduction--History. 3. Flowers--Folklore. I. Title.

SB407.S62 2004   582.13'09   C2003-904768-7

McClelland & Stewart Ltd.
The Canadian Publishers
481 University Avenue
Toronto, Ontario M5G 2E9
www.mcclelland.com

1 2 3 4 5 6 7 8 9 TWP 09 08 07 06 05 04 03
PRINTED AND BOUND IN SINGAPORE

Contents

Introduction

Most of us have been familiar with the flowers that appear in this book since we were children. When they bloom, we're able to name them without effort; many of us know where they like to be positioned in the garden and how to nurture them. Yet our knowledge of their origins and their pasts is sketchy at best. And why do we like some flowers more than others? Are our preferences influenced simply by a favorite color and a pleasant aroma, or are we attracted — sometimes repelled — by a distinct personality? Does the graceful-yet-sturdy iris, for example, actually communicate haughty independence, as some horticultural writers would have us believe? On reflection it seems that these ten "familiar" flowers, which we've encountered every year of our lives are, in fact, strangers. We know no more about them than of a new neighbor with whom we have only a nodding acquaintance.

This book aims to correct that situation. Each chapter is designed to increase our appreciation of a flower by explaining its origins — mythical and factual — and by recounting the adventures of the surprising people who found, collected and championed each plant so that it could eventually reach our gardens. Colorful personalities and significant events that have swirled around each flower are described in an attempt to reveal a plant's individuality and character. For example, when we learn that three women, well known at different times in history for their tragic-yet-momentous lives, were attracted to the dahlia, it's difficult not to wonder about the flower's melancholy charms.

I hope that, when you reach the last page of this book, these ten flowers will be as truly familiar as long-time friends or family members — and that there'll be ten fewer strangers in the garden.

ANDREW SMITH

A Little Respect

Revered by emperors, admired by gods, employed as a
symbol of royal strength, the chrysanthemum packs a powerful punch

Ponderous flower heads on sturdy stalks lend a venerable air to even the most riotously colored chrysanthemum beds. More often than not, cut chrysanthemums are surrounded by a reverent hush; in European cultures such as Italy and Greece, the large chrysanthemum flowers we sometimes call "mums" are employed exclusively to honor the dead. To display them at any other event but a funeral would be inappropriate. Chrysanthemums are viewed as such potent symbols of power and perfection by the Japanese, however, that at one time only the emperor was allowed to grow them. Even the diminutive European varieties, we sometimes affectionately call daisies, were admired by goddesses and included in royal insignia. It seems that wherever it raises its ray-like petals the charismatic chrysanthemum spells R-E-S-P-E-C-T.

Opposite: *Chrysanthemum* 'Sea Urchins'

AN OBJECT OF ORIENTAL ESTEEM 🐎

The deference that's always been accorded the chrysanthemum by the Chinese is expressed to this day at the annual Chrysanthemum Festival. The festival is said to have originated from the miraculous deliverance of a man and his family from certain death during the early part of the first millennium. Huan Jing was warned by Daoist priest Fei Chang-fang that on the ninth day of the ninth month his family would be in great danger. Fei recommended Huan tie a bag of dogwood to his arm, gather his family, and climb to a high place to drink chrysanthemum wine. Huan followed his advice. The next day, on returning home, Huan discovered that all living things, his pets, fowl, and livestock, had suffered mysterious violent deaths. Thanks to the priest's hill-climbing advice — not to mention the imbibing of chrysanthemum wine — the whole family survived.

The story of Huan Jing contains all the elements of the Chrysanthemum Festival as it's celebrated today. In September, when the plants bloom, friends and family members all over China climb a convenient hill and drink chrysanthemum wine to dispel evil and guarantee well-being for the year ahead. Chrysanthemum wine is thought to detoxify the body, help in weight loss, and be of benefit to the eyes. There's evidence that the chrysanthemums we commonly call "mums" originated and were hybridized in China — some of the species we grow today were written of admiringly by Confucius around 500 B.C.E.

By the fifth century the chrysanthemum, or *kiku* as it's called, had become a highly esteemed flower in Japan. It was so highly regarded that it was adopted as the personal symbol of the Mikado, the emperor. There were periods when nobody but the Imperial household was allowed to cultivate a chrysanthemum. A stylized representation of the single *Chrysanthemum* 'Hironishi,' a central disc with sixteen flaring petals, was adopted as the Imperial Standard in 1871.

At the end of the nineteenth century a European traveler described a chrysanthemum "viewing" by the Japanese royal party.

Chrysanthemum flowers appear to ride the waves on a Japanese ceramic bowl from the seventeenth-century Edo Period.

Slowly, and with great solemnity, the members of the court strolled down the paths lined by double rows of the army of flowers — graceful and elegant guards of honor — that filled the Imperial gardens. The entire festival had a severe, ceremonial, almost religious character.

Chrysanthemums are still viewed with reverence in Japan, from *Zukuri,* trained to produce hundreds of blooms, to *Ichimanji,* which bears only a single perfect flower.

THE GOLDEN FLOWER

The word chrysanthemum is derived from the Greek *chrysos* meaning gold, and *anthos* meaning flower. The Mediterranean *Chrysanthemum coronarium* is a yellow-golden flower and was sacred to Pallas Athena, the Greek goddess who was the patron of war, crafts, and manual skills. Flowering plants were fashioned into crowns, hence the name, and used during magic rituals designed to protect participants against demons. By the early seventeenth century, species of southern-European chrysanthemums had been transported north and west to England and France to be grown alongside native varieties. The tender *Chrysanthemum frutescens,* commonly called Paris daisy, is actually a native of the Canary Isles.

Several daisies from the chrysanthemum family bear the common name marguerite. *Chrysanthemum leucanthemum,* Ox-eye or Moon daisy, is called a marguerite in honor of a Frenchwoman, Marguerite of Anjou. She had a will of iron and was instrumental in regaining the English throne for her Lancastrian husband, Henry VI, when it was stolen by the opposing Yorkists during the fifteenth-century War of the Roses. A trinity of marguerites was embroidered on the robes and cloaks of all the members of her substantial household. Is it any wonder that a woman as strong-minded and regal as Marguerite of Anjou chose three sturdy chrysanthemum flowers as her badge?

A geisha admires huge chrysanthemum blooms at a flower festival in the Sendagi district of Tokyo, 1880. This print is the ninth print in a series titled "Twelve Months with the Boasts of Tokyo," created by Japanese artist Yoshitoshi.

THE ASIAN INVASION 🪳

Asian chrysanthemums are reported to have been grown in the Netherlands during the 1680s, but the first Chinese chrysanthemum to successfully join its European cousins was imported to France in 1789 by a Marseilles merchant, Monsieur Blanchard. Some reached England to be grown and developed successfully at the Royal Botanic Gardens, Kew. The horticultural site, often referred to as Kew Gardens, near Richmond in Surrey, was founded in 1759 by the widowed Augusta, Princess of Wales. Asian chrysanthemums were also grown in the botanical garden at the University of Pavia in Italy. However, it wasn't until after the Napoleonic Wars that Asian chrysanthemums overran Europe. Leading the charge was a retired soldier, M. Bernet of Toulouse. By 1825 the hybrids he grew and from which he gathered seed were the source of several new and valuable varieties. The old soldier named his chrysanthemums after brave comrades or for the battles in which they'd valiantly fought — catalogs of the time list chrysanthemums bearing names such as Bonaparte, Massena, Austerlitz, and Leipzig.

Chrysanthemum 'Little Rascal' (above) is a pompon, a variety named for its similarity to the tuft atop French sailors' berets.

Opposite: *Chrysanthemum indicum* painted by Mrs. Edward Roscoe (Margaret Lace) for the 1831 publication, *Floral Illustrations of the Seasons.*

Another wave of Asian chrysanthemums reached European shores in the remaining years of the nineteenth century. John Reeves, an Englishman employed by the East India Trading Company, was responsible for importing several varieties to Europe from China. One variety introduced was the "blush Ranunculus-flowered Chrysanthemum," called Drunken Lady by the Chinese on account of its rosy hue. In 1846, Scottish plant hunter Robert Fortune introduced the small-flowered Chusan daisy, popular in France (the varieties were named pompons after the tuft on the beret worn by French sailors). In 1851, thousands of pots of blooming chrysanthemums were used to decorate the Crystal Palace at the Great Exhibition in London. The island of Jersey in the Channel Isles, a huge producer of blooms for the flourishing cut-flower industry, cultivated more than four thousand different varieties of chrysanthemum.

It was during this time that chrysanthemums became associated with the dearly departed. Unlike most flowers, whose main prerequisite for blooming is sunshine,

This *Chrysanthemum indicum* appeared as "the yellow and white quilled Indian Marygold" in *Edwards's Botanical Register* of 1815.

many chrysanthemum plants also need at least twelve hours of darkness in order to blossom. Hence their autumn flowering, after the summer solstice when nights are longer. Since late chrysanthemum flowers became available in abundance around November 2, All Souls' Day, which is traditionally a day for remembering the dead in many European cultures, they were soon liberally used to decorate family graves in the early winter, and the chrysanthemum quickly became the flower of mourning in the minds of millions of people. When modern growing techniques made them available throughout the year, they were used to decorate coffins no matter what the month. Now, in countries such as Italy and Greece, it's considered bad taste to display them at any event other than a funeral.

CHRYSANTHEMUMS IN THE NEW WORLD

Most of the members of the chrysanthemum family have made the trip to North America. The pompon varieties were popular in the Eastern states at the end of the 1800s. Despite their hardiness, chrysanthemum flowers often needed protection from the icy autumnal blasts of New England. It was common for worn-out clothes

HOW THE CHRYSANTHEMUM NAME WAS LOST ... AND FOUND

Carl von Linné, or Carolus Linnaeus, as he became known, was the Swedish botanist who, in the 1730s, took upon himself the staggering burden of grouping and naming all known plants. One wonders at the ego of the man; he intended his taxonomic system to describe all living things from algae to animals. Others before and since have evolved classification methods, but the double Latin label system (genus followed by species) that Linnaeus developed has been generally accepted as common garden parlance worldwide. In the eighteenth century, a plant was brought from Asia that struck Linnaeus as being similar in form and flower to the southern European corn marigold, *Chrysanthemum segetum*. He therefore christened the new plant *Chrysanthemum indicum*. Other plants similar to the corn marigold were also considered by Linnaeus as belonging to the same genus; Feverfew, for example, was given the scientific name *Chrysanthemum parthenium*.

Then, after 250 years in the life of the chrysanthemum family, Nickolae Tzvelev, a Russian botanist, decided that Linnaeus had been wrong, and that the different flowers were not similar enough to be grouped under the same first name. As a result, the family was separated; Feverfew was renamed *Tanacetum parthenium* and the Asian chrysanthemum, or mums as they had come to be called, were given the moniker *Dendranthema x grandiflorum*.

Confusion reigned. Dutch growers increasingly referred to *Dendranthema,* but everyone else downright refused. Finally the International Botanical Congress, the authority that determines scientific plant names, had had enough. They ruled that garden mums should be reunited with their family and revert to their original and appropriately stately name — *Chrysanthemum*.

Swedish taxonomist Carl von Linné (shown here in a Lapp costume) decreed that three similar plants would all become members of the chrysanthemum family. Others since have begged to differ, but what Linnaeus — as he became known — decreed is almost impossible to reverse. His classification system, Latin genus name followed by species, has become the universal language of gardeners.

15

Opposite:
Chrysanthemum coccineum 'Painted Daisy'

to be spread over late-blooming plants at night to prolong their flowering time; from contemporary reports, it seems the garment of preference was grandma's red flannel petticoat.

The importation of the chrysanthemum group known as the "Hairy Japanese" is credited to a grateful Japanese man. In 1864, twenty-one-year-old Shimeta Neesima begged a working passage from Shanghai on a Boston-bound ship, the *Wild Rover*. The young Neesima was eager to reach America to continue religious studies in Christianity, begun secretly back home in Japan where the Christian church was banned. Mr. and Mrs. Alpheus Hardy, owners of the *Wild Rover*, heard about the plucky Japanese convert and sought out Neesima on his arrival in Boston. So impressed was Hardy, who as a young man had aspired to be a theologian himself, that he offered to pay for the young man's studies. In 1874, Neesima graduated from Amherst College in science and theology due in large part to the Hardys' generosity. He returned to Japan, where Christianity was now tolerated, as a missionary. Out of respect and gratitude to Captain and Mrs. Hardy, who was a keen gardener, he sent some Japanese chrysanthemums to his American benefactors. Mrs. Hardy nurtured the plants and eventually produced blooms which she showed at a Boston flower show in November 1887. The catalog reads:

> It is also pleasant to record the fact that an entirely new group of flowers has reached us from Japan, having been sent to Mrs. Alpheus Hardy, by Neesima, a native of Japan, out of gratitude to Mrs. Hardy for favors shown him while in this country. One of the last mentioned collection has been named Mrs. Alpheus Hardy. It is a beautiful, large incurved Japanese variety, having feathery petals of wonderful delicacy and whiteness, and is the most sumptuous of the whole family thus far known.

AN INSECTICIDE GIANT

A small chrysanthemum that packs a powerful punch is *Chrysanthemum cinerariifolium*, also known as pyrethrum. Although pyrethrum flowers had been used as an insecticide in Persia for centuries, it was little known elsewhere until the end of the nineteenth century. It's said to have been rediscovered when a resourceful German woman living in Dubrovnik threw a bouquet of wildflowers she had picked into a corner after they had withered. Several weeks later she noticed the dried flowers were surrounded by dead insects. She researched the insecticidal properties of the flowers and began to manufacture pyrethrum as a commercial product.

A native of Dalmatia, the plant is now grown all over the world as a source of insecticide. Its flowers are made into a powder and sold under various trade names. One of its first uses was to spray the inside of airplanes to prevent the transference of insects, particularly mosquitoes, from country to country. It's been claimed that pyrethrum is fifteen times more toxic to adult mosquitoes than DDT. The beauty of pyrethrum as an insecticide is that it's believed to be ecologically sound — harmless to people and the environment in general.

In the melting pot milieu of 1880s California, Luther Burbank used a mix of native and foreign chrysanthemums to develop the Shasta daisy. The admiration he felt for the flower is reflected in its Latin names, Chrysanthemum superbum *and* Chrysanthemum maximum.

The whole stock of *Chrysanthemum* 'Mrs. Alpheus Hardy' was bought by a local grower for the princely sum of $1,500. The investment must have paid off handsomely two years later, when a large consignment was shipped to eager growers in Europe.

At the end of the nineteenth century, the American melting-pot mentality came into play with the development of a chrysanthemum peculiar to the United States. Luther Burbank of California labored for several years, using varieties of chrysanthemum from Europe and Japan, as well as native plants, to develop his Shasta daisy, *Chrysanthemum superbum* or *Chrysanthemum maximum,* commonly known as the Shasta daisy, named after sparkling white Mount Shasta in California. Burbank respectfully described the shasta as "a plant at once graceful enough to please the eye and hardy enough to grow in any soil . . . a daisy that surpasses any dreams."

Below: Luther Burbank's Shasta daisy, *Chrysanthemum superbum,* or *Chrysanthemum maximum,* as it's also known.

WEED SANDWICHES END A WIFE'S MIGRAINE

In 1978, a London newspaper, *The Sunday Express*, ran a headline that announced: "Weed sandwiches end a wife's migraine." The "wife" in question was Mrs. Ann Jenkins, whose husband was a Welsh doctor, which doubtless added credence to her story. The "weed" of the headline was Feverfew, *Chrysanthemum parthenium*. The newspaper went on to describe how Mrs. Jenkins cured her migraine with a regular snack of sandwiches filled with Feverfew leaves. *The Sunday Express* reported: "Four years ago she looked so frail and ill that neighbours wished there was something — anything — they could do to help. But today Mrs. Jenkins is an elegant woman in her late sixties, full of health and energy."

She wasn't the first to be helped by this potent chrysanthemum. In the first century, Plutarch claimed that Feverfew was used to save the life of a worker who fell from the Parthenon during its construction, which explains the origin of its Latin nomenclature. *Chrysanthemum parthenium* has a host of fanciful common names — Featherfoil, Flirtwort, and Nosebleed. The French know it as *Grande Chamomille*. Feverfew has been used throughout history to treat a variety of ailments such as fevers, migraine, difficulties of childbirth, threatened miscarriage, as well as for the relief of toothache, stomachache, insect-bite itch, and arthritis pain. The use of Feverfew was once so widespread that it's been described as the "Aspirin of the eighteenth century." In 1772, Dr. John Hill, a British physician, wrote, "in the worst headaches this herb exceeds whatever else is known."

Since Mrs. Jenkins's well-publicized experience, bolstered by positive evidence from medical studies of Feverfew reported in such respectable sources as *Lancet* and the *British Medical Journal*, a host of natural-remedy companies have started to produce Feverfew tablets, capsules, and essences. These allow the user to take Feverfew without the risk of mouth ulcers, sometimes a side effect of eating Feverfew leaves. The plant is known to induce miscarriage and abortion in cows, so it's probably not wise for pregnant women to dabble with Feverfew, and there are no long-term studies that identify side effects associated with continual ingestion.

However, with a spoonful of sugar to help the medicine go down — because the leaves are unappetizingly bitter a sweetener is often added — Mrs. Jenkins and thousands of others have found relief for what ails them from this powerful little chrysanthemum.

Opposite: *Chrysanthemum indicum* from *Curtis's Botanical Magazine.*

Below: *Chrysanthemum parthenium*, or Feverfew, once described as the "Aspirin of the eighteenth century."

Crazy for Clematis

Many are besotted by the charms of clematis vines.
But beware, the clematis can be hurtful

The clematis eventually wends its way into the affections of anybody who encounters it. The plant's sinuous habit and profusion of blooms made it a favorite of ancient hedonist Bacchus. The open demeanor of clematis flowers is said to evoke joy and a light heart. It's little wonder flowering clematis vines were woven into crowns and garlands used in celebratory processions and festivals. When people fall for clematis, they fall hard. Miss Ellen Willmott spent a considerable fortune creating a garden in the south of England filled almost entirely with clematis plants. Famed garden designer Gertrude Jekyll used the gently twisting clematis to ramp over other plants whose flowering season was finished. But some clematis plants are best worshipped from afar, for their sap can be harmful to the skin.

Opposite: *Clematis* 'Nelly Moser'

UNIVERSALLY ADORED

Given its range, the clematis seems to entwine the entire temperate world. Native varieties wind their way through North America, Europe, and Asia. Wild clematis can be found in Africa, Australia, and New Zealand. One of the earliest reports of its cultivation in Europe comes from the Greek botanist Pedanios Dioscorides around 50 A.D. He is thought to have originated the name — from the Greek *klema* meaning a tendril, shoot, or vine — which was then used by the younger Pliny to describe the plant in his *Historia Naturalis*.

At the end of the sixteenth century, Hugh Morgan, an English pharmacist attached to the court of Queen Elizabeth I, managed to develop various colors of *Clematis viticella* in his garden. At the same time, medieval English herbalist John Gerard praised the native *Clematis vitalba* for, "the beautie of the flowers, and the pleasant scent or savour of the same." He even found the seed heads of the plant uplifting in winter, "its goodly shewe . . . covering the hedges white all over with his fetherlike tops." It was during the Elizabethan reign that clematis became known as Ladies' Bower or Virgin's Bower, which Gerard attributes to its "aptness in making of arbors, bowers and shadie couertures." Italians named clematis *barbagrigia*, "gray beard," and in England it's sometimes called Hedge Feathers, both names evocative of clematis's fluffy seed heads.

Throughout the eighteenth century, different varieties of clematis were exchanged by gardeners across Europe. One of the most distant sources was Siberia. British horticulturist Philip Miller, curator of the Chelsea Physic Garden during the 1700s, described *Clematis sibirica* in his *Gardener's Dictionary*:

> *This plant grows naturally in Tartary, where it was discovered by Dr. Gmelin, who sent the seeds to the Imperial Garden at Petersburg, where they succeeded; and in 1753 I was favoured with some of the seeds of that Garden, which have succeeded at Chelsea.*

The first Asian clematis to reach Europe seems to have been *Clematis florida*, introduced from Japan in 1776 by the Quaker physician and plant collector Dr. John Fothergill. His famous garden in Upton, Essex, was so stuffed with the diverse spoils of globe-trotting plant collectors that it was reported "the sphere seemed transposed, and the Arctic Circle joined the Equator." In the 1820s, Lady Amherst,

Opposite: *Clematis montana* from *Edwards's Botanical Register*, 1815.

a keen gardener and the wife of then-governor general of India, William Pitt Amherst, brought home to England from India the stunning white-blooming *Clematis montana*. However, the most momentous clematis import to Europe was achieved thanks to a momentous horticultural discovery, used to great advantage by the intrepid plant hunter Robert Fortune.

A NOT-SO-SMALL MIRACLE

The plant collector's greatest problem was the nourishment of living specimens on long sea voyages. Fresh water was a valuable commodity at sea; captains were reluctant to ask crews to go thirsty so that a bunch of greenery could be kept alive. In the early nineteenth century, Nathaniel Bagshaw Ward, a doctor practising in the East End of London, stumbled across a solution to this age-old problem. Although Dr. Ward lived in the center of the city, Welcome Square, near London docks, he was a keen naturalist. During one of his trips to the countryside surrounding London, he found a chrysalis, which he brought home with the intention of observing it hatch. Dr. Ward buried the chrysalis in some earth on a flat container and covered the earth with a glass jar. After a while he noticed that seeds had germinated inside the jar. Soon shoots of plants that wouldn't normally live for five minutes in the stale air of a London house were perkily poking up from the earth inside the jar. On further inspection, Nathaniel Ward observed that moisture evaporating from the earth and vegetation had formed condensation on the inside surfaces of the jar. Drops of water ran down the glass and back into the soil to moisten it. And so the cycle continued, creating a self-sufficient, independent atmosphere in which plants thrived.

Dr. Ward was soon growing a host of moisture-loving plants under virtually airtight glass containers. Fern gardens grown in this way soon became a Victorian novelty. With no effort, people were able to cultivate diminutive Gardens of Eden at home despite the coal and gas fumes of their living rooms. It wasn't long until the Horticultural Society of England realized the potential of glazed traveling cases for protecting living plants from the salt air and changeable temperatures of long sea journeys. The person chosen to test these miraculous traveling cases was the renowned plant hunter Robert Fortune.

Opposite: This invention, as shown in Nathianiel Bagshaw Ward's *On the Growth of Plants in Closely Glazed Cases,* supplied safe passage to *Clematis lanuginosa* on its voyage to England from China.

Clematis lanuginosa *was one of the first plants to be exported to Europe from Asia by means of the miraculous Wardian case. Other triumphs of the device that sustained plants on long sea voyages were the introduction of Chinese tea plants to India and the importation of the Asian banana tree to the Americas.*

Left: Nathaniel
Bagshaw Ward's
invention was all the
rage in Victorian
parlours, where it
sheltered fern gardens,
independent and self-
sustaining within their
sealed glass case.

Opposite:
Clematis 'Niobe'

ADVENTURES OF A PLANT HUNTER 🏃

Fortune was a Scot, born in Berwickshire in 1812. After an apprenticeship and jobs in various gardens in his native Scotland, he was selected for one of the British Botanical Society's plant-collecting expeditions. He was required to sign a demanding contract for a year's work in China for the paltry sum of £100 (he received five times that amount from the East India Company for his second trip to China a few years later). In February 1843, Fortune embarked on the *Emu* bound for Hong Kong. The ship was loaded with Wardian cases, as Nathaniel Ward's glass boxes had been named, stuffed with European plants bound for the new colony. The fact that every plant arrived in Hong Kong alive and healthy augured well for Fortune's mission in China.

But a plant hunter's life is never easy. Fortune was appalled by what he called "the deplorable condition" of Hong Kong — "fever was rife and bands of robbers roamed the streets at night." He'd been told that further up the coast near Ning Po he'd find a landscape rich in vegetation. He set sail as soon as he could, intent on stocking his Wardian cases with new and exotic flora. At stops along the way, the Presbyterian Scot continued to be shocked by the conditions of the country: "Many of the northern cities, evidently once in the most flourishing condition, are now in a state of decay." Fortune's vessel was caught in a violent monsoon storm with waves so wild that a thirty-pound fish was thrown out of the sea and crashed through a skylight to land on a table in front of a startled sailor. Once the wind abated, Fortune was dismayed to discover that two of his Wardian cases had been destroyed.

When the ship dropped anchor at the nearest coast for the crew to mend sails and carry out repairs, Fortune decided to explore the local countryside. On the way

Below: *Clematis x jackmanii* and *Clematis* 'Comtesse de Bouchard', both hybrids created using Fortune's imports.

back to the ship, carrying a few choice plants, he and his servant were surrounded by a throng of people. Fortune felt a hand in his pocket and realized he was being robbed. Meanwhile his servant had been accosted by a group of natives wielding knives: "They threatened to stab him if he offered the least resistance, at the same time endeavouring to rob and strip him, and my poor plants collected with so much care were flying in all directions." Fortune and his servant managed to escape unharmed by giving up all their valuables.

The trials of his journey were rewarded when Fortune finally arrived at Ning Po, where he was entranced by the rich display of vegetation found on the towering peaks and sloping valleys of the surrounding area. He describes azaleas of "dazzling brightness and surpassing beauty. Wild roses, honeysuckles . . . and a hundred others, mingle their flowers with them, and make us confess that China is indeed the 'central flowery land.'" Most Europeans, including Fortune, were only familiar with European and North American clematis plants, which have comparatively small flowers. When Fortune first caught sight of a blooming *Clematis lanuginosa* studded with

On May 6, 1846, plant collector Robert Fortune sailed triumphantly up the River Thames with varieties of Asian clematis plants that boasted much larger blooms than any clematis in the West. Fortune reported on the hard-won spoils of his three years in China: "The plants arrived in excellent order, and were immediately conveyed to the garden of the Horticultural Society at Chiswick."

massive flowers, his heart must have soared and the hardships of his journey melted away. Another traveler in China at the time describes *Clematis lanuginosa* growing "on the stony slopes supporting itself on low bushes. The huge azure blue flowers caught the eye from afar."

After Fortune returned safely to Hong Kong, he wasted no time in setting sail for home.

> *Eighteen glazed cases, filled with the most beautiful plants of northern China, were placed upon the poop of the ship and we sailed on the 22d of December. After a long but favourable voyage, we anchored in the Thames, on the 6th of May, 1846. The plants arrived in excellent order, and were immediately conveyed to the garden of the Horticultural Society at Chiswick.*

Thanks to Robert Fortune's perseverance *Clematis lanuginosa* was used to hybridize large-flowered plants that radically altered the appearance of the clematis in the West. The innovation of the Wardian case was responsible for the exportation of a huge number of plants from their native countries to new homes around the world. Just two, the Chinese tea plant and the Asian banana, made immense personal fortunes for plantation owners in India and the Americas. There is no record however that Dr. Nathaniel Ward made anything but a modest sum from his globe-altering discovery.

AN OBJECT OF PASSION ࣫

Mr. Ernest Markham, head gardener of the famous late-nineteenth-century British garden at Gravetye Manor, was so fond of clematis that a plant was named for him when a traditionally lavender-colored flower turned up pink. It was labeled *Clematis macropetala var. markhamii*. Markham's employer, William Robinson, an ardent proponent of the so-called "natural" garden, shared his gardener's passion for clematis plants. Robinson, reputed to be irascible and quarrelsome, spoke warmly of the clematis: ". . . hardy as the oak . . . come early into flower and only cease with the approach of winter. Of few other flowers can this be said."

Present-day British garden expert Christopher Lloyd describes his

Opposite: In the 1800s, *Curtis's Botanical Magazine* captioned this illustration as "*Clematis crispa*, curled-flowered Virgin's-bower."

A pink clematis entwines this art nouveau glass vase by Auguste Daum of Nancy.

fondness for clematis: "I love nearly all of them, even the tiniest and most insignificant in their different ways, and all for their fascinating diversity of habit, colour and flower form."

But the most passionate liaison with the clematis was a family affair. In 1858, Jackman's nursery, run by the Jackman family of Woking, England, produced *Clematis x jackmanii*, a showy plant with generous, rich, blue-purple flowers on new growth. The vine, thought to be a cross between Robert Fortune's *Clematis lanuginosa* and the dark European *Clematis viticella*, caused a sensation when exhibited in 1863. Since then most people's first encounter with clematis is with the ubiquitous *Clematis x jackmanii*.

The Jackman family's subsequent development of countless clematis varieties was the beginning of a wave of clematis hybridization that swept Europe, resulting in hundreds of varieties. However, passions ran high when the natural single flower

Below: The large, rich, blue-purple flowers of *Clematis x jackmanii* caused a sensation when it was first exhibited in 1863.

THE CLEMATIS CAN BE HURTFUL

Certain varieties of clematis have been known as *Herbae Flammula Jovis,* "herbs with the small fire of Jupiter." So described because the leaves, when crushed, secrete an irritating juice, which burns the skin and can cause blistering. If rubbed into a small cut in the skin, the sap of some clematis can cause a large superficial sore. Nineteenth-century botanist Anne Pratt accuses these clematis in her book, *"Poisonous, Noxious, and Suspected Plants of Our Fields and Woods,"* of being "acrimonious." She quotes Philip Miller, who wrote in 1722: "If one leaf be dropped on a hot day in the summer and bruised . . . it will cause pain like a flame . . . and the fresh leaves are used by beggars to cause wounds in order to excite compassion." Records of clematis being used in this manner by mendicants to gain sympathy go back as far as the reign of Roman Emperor Nero, early in the first century.

It's for this reason that the unfortunate meaning attached to clematis in most languages of flowers is artifice. "Trust not the Clematis!" the French author A. Grandville warns. "[It] climbs slyly up the walls, and shows her little head at the edge of the window, where young maidens go at evening to talk. The artful Clematis gets possession of their secrets."

---

form was changed to a double. Victorian garden writer Sir Herbert Maxwell expressed his dislike for double versions of clematis when he wrote:

> *No milder epithet suffices as the distortion of a perfect flower into a monstrosity that can only merit the kind of moribund attention bestowed on a two-headed calf or a four-legged chicken in a village museum.*

The clematis is not only admired for its flowers, but also for its remarkably tough stems. In North and South America and in Asia, it's been used as rope. French peasant women made clotheslines from clematis vine. Ancient Romans fashioned clematis baskets. The Masai tribe of East Africa and some native North Americans use crushed leaves of native clematis as snuff. However, it's not advisable to stuff just any clematis leaf up one's nose, since some varieties can cause damaging skin irritation (see box above). *Clematis vitalba* stems can be smoked like cigarettes and are said to give a good puff without catching fire. In England it's been called Smoking Cane or Gypsies' Bacca. But *Clematis vitalba* has another use: in Russia and Italy, young shoots are boiled in water and eaten like asparagus.

For most of us, clematis vines are treasured for their beautiful appearance and as an uplifting spirit raiser. Herbalist John Gerard summed it up when he named the wild clematis which festooned hedgerows along medieval English lanes. He called it Traveller's-Joy, "by reason of the goodly show and the pleasant scent or savour of its flowers, and because of its decking waies . . . where people travel."

Ever the Optimist

Its favorite civilization destroyed by a cataclysm, exposed as an impotent panacea, the plucky crocus keeps on blooming

There's something heart-achingly stoic about a spring crocus. It stands, often bowed by snow and ice, striving to convey optimism, its duty to bring encouraging promise of imminent vigor to the winter-weary. Then some lout of a bird passes by and snaps off its petals, apparently just for fun, and litters the surrounding snow with shards of yellow or purple. But what can be expected of a flower whose mythical namesake received a fatal blow to the head with a discus?

Opposite: *Crocus vernus*

Opposite: In the seventeenth-century, when Jacob Jordaens painted this representation of Europa, the mother of Crocus, being carried off by Zeus, he included tiny crocus flowers in her wreath, doubtless an allusion to her dead son.

BORN OUT OF TRAGEDY ?

According to ancient Greek mythology, the crocus flower originated on a day when the gods were amusing themselves by racing each other to prove who was the fastest runner. However, for Hermes, whose winged feet made him the assured winner every time, racing was tedious. In his boredom, Hermes idly threw a discus, paying no attention to where it might land. The discus hit Crocus, the infant son of Europa, killing the lad instantly. Drops of the boy's blood fell on the surrounding ground. Hermes, full of anguish and remorse, transformed Crocus's spilt blood into flowers. After her son's death, Europa was seldom seen without a crocus flower. Lord Alfred Tennyson, the English romantic poet, once described her:

Sweet Europa's mantle blew unclasped
From off her shoulder, backward borne,
From one hand drooped a crocus, one hand grasped
The mild bull's golden horn.

A more down-to-earth explanation for the naming of the plant is that Greeks would have heard renderings of the word for the flower — *krkm* — in ancient languages of Mesopotamia, in which consonants were emphasized more than vowels. Thus evolved the Greek word *krokos*. Homer describes it as the "flaming crocus [that] made the mountain glow."

THE CROCUS AND THE VOLCANO ?

The plant is probably as old as the Mediterranean hills on which it can be found growing wild. Representations of crocus abound in paintings, murals, and crafts of many ancient Mediterranean cultures. A four-thousand-year-old clay pot, probably used for storing liquids, decorated with red and white crocus flowers, was found during the excavation of an archaeological site in Crete. The crocus is depicted so often and so prominently in the Minoan civilization of Crete that it's obvious the flower was more than just a decoration.

Around 2000 B.C.E., stylish Minoan women were wearing full skirts with depictions of crocus flowers sprouting from their hems and waists. The neckline of these tight-wasted garments, probably votive robes used during religious rites, plunged so low that the wearer's breasts were proudly exposed. By this time the

Crocus's mother, Europa, didn't seem to take much solace in the fact that the
splattered blood of Crocus, her dead infant son, gave rise to a pretty little flower.
She was eventually carried off by Zeus in the form of a bull.

39

Minoans were growing crocuses as a source of saffron, a valuable spice that must have contributed greatly to the Cretan economy. The dedication to the collection of crocus flowers is obvious in a mural that takes up a whole wall in the Palace of Knossus in Crete. The mural depicts a tall figure picking stylized crocuses, their flowers unnaturally swollen and the length of stamens and stigmas exaggerated. Bowls filled with crocus flowers are dotted among rocks surrounding the figure. Although stained and damaged, the painting is still imbued with a promise of plenitude; the energetic crocuses add a sense of optimistic exuberance to the landscape.

Sixty miles away, on the Mediterranean island of Santorini, once part of a larger island called Thera, ancient murals depict the crocus in such a way that it's clear the flower was especially important to Theran women. Many of the murals uncovered in the four-thousand-year-old town of Akrotiri on Santorini show young women either picking crocuses or with crocus flowers woven or embroidered on their clothes. Their robes are made from cloth dyed saffron yellow. Some scholars go so far as to suggest that young women in one Theran mural display proof of a saffron-rich diet because of blue streaks in their eyes (a sign of a diet rich in riboflavins and carotene found in saffron), whereas the red-streaked eyes of the men and older women reveal a lack of riboflavin. The inference is that only fertile women — the promise of society's continuation — were allowed to consume saffron and to be associated with the crocus. It's clear that at least one Theran beekeeper was optimistic about gathering saffron honey when a beehive, recently unearthed on Santorini, was found to be decorated with crocus flowers.

For centuries the islands of Crete and Thera were home to peace-loving, gentle people for whom the crocus held sacred and secular significance. However, in the seventeenth century B.C.E. both cultures were obliterated in a matter of days by massive forces of nature. A spectacular volcanic eruption on Thera, which scientists believe was five times more powerful than Krakatoa, was responsible for the destruction of Theran society. So wide was the resulting crater that the volcano folded in on itself, forming an archipelago of islands out of the original single island of Thera. It's thought that the devastating volcanic damage that destroyed Thera was also the last blow to the Minoans of nearby Crete, already

Opposite: *Crocus vernus* 'King of Striped'

The elongated figure, picking crocuses in this four-thousand-year-old Cretan mural, was originally reconstructed as a boy, but other Minoan murals, unearthed at Knossus and Akrotiri, have given historians reason to believe that the figure was actually a monkey.

decimated by a series of powerful earthquakes. Crete was doubtless covered by a rain of falling ash from the eruption on Thera that would have darkened the skies for days. Tidal waves carried Cretan ships miles inland. The crocuses of Thera would have been destroyed; all that remained was a desolate landscape of smoking pumice and volcanic dust. It's fortunate for the crocus that plants survived on the Greek mainland, in Turkey, and in North Africa.

A HOT GLOWING COAL OF FIRE 🦂

Although most of the eighty recognized species of crocus grow naturally in the Mediterranean region, some can be found as far east as China, as far north as Poland, and as far south as Jordan and Iran. As people roamed further afield, the crocus was introduced to countries outside of its natural habitat. Persians are known to have taken the plant to the Indian subcontinent, where it became a favorite of the people of Kashmir.

The crocus was introduced to England during the reign of Queen Elizabeth I. Its first mention in the late sixteenth century belongs to the medieval herbalist John Gerard, who wrote: "That pleasant plant that bringeth forth yellow floures was sent unto me from Robinus of Paris." Gerard is referring to Jean Robin, nurseryman to the king of France, whom Gerard much admired for his botanical successes at the Jardin des Plants. Gerard described crocus flowers as being "of a most perfect shining yellow colour, seeming afar off to be a hot glowing cole of fire."

In Ireland the crocus is traditionally a St. Valentine's flower. It blooms early to greet the saint on his day, February 14. It was a custom in Ireland to pick yellow crocus flowers to place on St. Valentine's shrine. The purple-colored, however, were left unpicked to provide shelter for fairies, who were said to prefer them over the yellow crocus.

By the seventeenth century, the crocuses of European florists could be had large or small in solid white, purple, pale or deep yellow, and with striped or flamed petals. Dutch growers threw themselves into the development of the crocus with almost as much zeal as for the tulip. By the 1750s, one could buy "100 Roots and 12 Sorts for 1 Guilder." England developed a large bulb-growing industry centered in an area of Lincolnshire known as Little Holland. One wonders if the region was named so that allegations could be made as to the origin of its crocuses and tulips. George Maw, the crocus-loving Victorian industrialist, who wrote extensively on the subject, quotes a contemporary claim that "at least nine-tenths of the Dutch bulbs which are advertised annually as 'just imported from Holland' are from Holland in Lincolnshire, and are guiltless of any connection with Holland on the mainland of the continent of Europe."

Late-flowering varieties have never proved as popular as the early crocuses. Perhaps autumn, with its guarantee of inevitable winter to follow, is just too overwhelming — a crocus seems somehow inappropriate. John Parkinson, author of the 1629 horticultural bible *Paradisi in Sole Paradisus Terrestris,* described these autumn-flowering plants as "having a spring-like appearance [that] puts you in mind of that reviving season, [at a time] when Nature, in other respects, seems to be in total decay."

Corms of spring crocuses were transported to North America by settlers, symbols of optimism for a New World. Those that survived ships' rodents — crocus

A nineteenth-century painting of *Crocus speciosus*, an autumn-flowering variety.

43

The saffron crocus was so valuable in some cultures that the death penalty was common for anyone trying to pass off a lesser plant as the genuine item. In Egypt, saffron was prescribed, mixed with worm's blood and scribe's excrement, to make a healing ointment.

the true Saffron.

corms are a delicacy for mice and rats — were planted at the entrances of frontier log cabins and prairie sod houses. Despite the North American late-winter chill, clumps of crocuses flowered selflessly to bring hopeful good cheer to hunters and farmers returning cold and exhausted to their pioneer homes.

GOOD AS GOLD 🏃

The crocus's strength is in numbers — crocus flowers can be breathtaking en masse. And a mass is what's needed when it comes to gathering enough blooms to produce the wondrous spice known as saffron, from the Arabic word *zafaran*. Saffron is the dried stigmas of autumn-flowering *Crocus sativus* — not to be confused with colchicum, an autumn flower that's similar in appearance (see page 47). Because more than four thousand flowers of *Crocus sativus* are needed to make an ounce of saffron, the spice has been valuable throughout history, sometimes worth more than its weight in gold.

Considering that modern studies have proved that saffron has little or no medical value, it's astonishing that the spice was considered by so many cultures to be such an effective medicine. Two extensive documents claim it as a wonder drug. The first is *Papyrus Ebers*, named for the German who found it, an Egyptian medical scroll of around 1550 B.C.E., thought to be a copy of a more ancient document. Saffron is mentioned as an ingredient in everything from poultices to ointments to eye drops. But then, so is scribe's excrement, toes-of-a-dog, and worm's blood.

Not much had changed when, in 1671, John Ferdinand Hertodt published *Crocologia*, a massive three-hundred-page volume singing the virtues of saffron as a medicine. Melancholia, poisonous bites, dental pain, and insanity — even the plague — were said to be cured by an application of saffron in some form or other. As in ancient Egypt, it was necessary to add saffron to bizarre ingredients such as fat of a mouse, swallow's nest, and dragon's blood.

The addition of saffron to alcohol was believed to protect against hangovers. Perhaps that's why ancient Romans hung garlands of fresh *Crocus sativus* around goblets of wine. The sixteenth-century botanist William Turner, who could obviously hold his liquor, said that saffron was "good for weak braynes that cannot well beare drinke."

Opposite: Christoph Jacob Trew's 1750 illustration of *Crocus sativus*.

45

Saffron was probably more effective as a deodorant. In the latter days of the Roman Empire, when excess took place every day, banquet halls were drenched in the scent of saffron. Slaves covered floors with lashings of dried stigmas mixed with vermilion and powdered mica. The result was a sparkling crimson carpet that emanated the slightly antiseptic smell of saffron. The Romans didn't stop there in the use of saffron — they included it in their cuisine. According to the *Satyricon of Petronius Arbiter*, cakes were served shaped like fruits.

We applied ourselves to this dessert and our joviality was suddenly revived by a fresh diversion, for at the smallest pressure the cakes squirted a saffron sauce upon us, and even spurted unpleasantly in our faces.

Given the Romans' love of saffron, it's reasonable to believe that they introduced *Crocus sativus* to the rest of Europe. However, a story persists, told by the sixteenth-century geographer Richard Hakluyt, of its reintroduction to England by a traveler.

At Algiers a pilgrim stole beads [corms] of saffron and hid them in his Palmer's staff which he had made hollow before of purpose, and so he brought this root to this realm, with venture of his life; for if he had been taken, by law of the country from whence it came, he had died for the fact.

The threat of death is no exaggeration. There were many who lost their lives for either stealing saffron or trying to pass off similar substances as the genuine item. In the city of Nuremberg, Germany, a merchant, Jobst Findeker, who was caught hawking adulterated saffron in 1444, was burnt along with his tainted wares. Nuremberg had became one of the main centers for the trading of saffron. So important was the spice to the economy of the city that inspectors, known as *Safranschauers,* were appointed to help enforce laws designed to keep strict control on the quality of saffron sold. Miscreants were severely punished, evisceration was common, and some of the guilty were buried alive.

Henry I of England was so fond of saffron as a spice that he forbade what he considered to be the wasteful use of it by ladies of the court to lighten their hair. At the time saffron was believed to be such a powerful antiseptic that it wasn't deemed necessary to launder saffron-dyed sheets. Another use is described by a sixteenth-century writer, "Saffron killeth moths if it be sowed in paper bags

MEADOW SAFFRON AND NAKED LADIES

The flower of the colchicum corm is so similar to that of *Crocus sativus*, the bloom from which saffron is harvested, that it's been called Meadow Saffron. The flower of the colchicum is more open than that of a crocus, the petals separate from each other. Colchicum flowers can be white but are most commonly pale purple or rose-colored. Colchicums are sometimes called Naked Ladies, because the flowers appear on bare stalks, after the plant's foliage has died off in late summer.

Native to an area near the Black Sea, once the site of an ancient civilization called Colchis, the plant has been used for centuries as a source of poison. According to Greek mythology, Medea used colchicum to poison her enemies. The freshly cut corms smell like radish, but on first taste are sweet and then quickly become bitter. The Greek physician and botanist Dioscorides described its modus operandi: "It killeth by choking." The alkaloid ingredient colchinine acts upon secreting organs and depresses the heart and lungs. Symptoms are choking, severe cramping, and vomiting. In very small quantities, colchicum has been used as a medicine. It's reputed to alleviate the pain of gout and rheumatism. Externally, colchicum has proved an effective antidote to fleas, and a mixture of water and flowers is said to be good for the complexion.

Colchine (sometimes called colchicine), extracted from colchicum corms, is used by horticulturists to restore fertility to sterile plants. Colchine has the ability to render a sterile hybrid fertile by increasing the number of chromosomes in a plant's cells.

---

verie thin, and laid up in presses amongst tapestrie or apparel."

The British town of Saffron Walden became synonymous with the production of saffron. Locals made vast fortunes. Audley End, one of the great houses of England, was built in the countryside near Saffron Walden with profits garnered from locally grown saffron. But the death knell began to toll for saffron in the early 1900s. The formulation of man-made dyes had rendered the purchase of expensive saffron dye unnecessary. Its medical powers were discredited. It wasn't long before the production of saffron became unprofitable.

Saffron is still used widely for cooking — in Cornwall, it flavors saffron bread, in Marseilles, it heightens the tastes of bouillabaisse, and in Spain, it colors paella an appetizing gold.

Above: *Colchicum*, misleadingly known as Meadow Saffron.

Curse of the Dahlia

Bloody human sacrifices, a duped smuggler, and a possessive empress mark the dahlia's stormy passage to fame and fortune

Some people find dahlias distasteful. Their fulsome blooms, top-heavy with an excess of petals, are considered vulgar. Although there's nothing intrinsically perilous about the dahlia — a dose of dermatitis from prolonged handling of its tubers is as harmful as the plant gets — the conspicuous flaunting of so much provocative beauty can evoke a sense of foreboding. Perhaps the flower, nurtured and loved by tragic Empress Josephine, who traded on her looks but lost Napoleon, is destined to be suffused forever with her jealous melancholy. Maybe its roots were too deeply immersed in the blood of Aztec human sacrifices. Certainly the brutal destruction of a sophisticated civilization paved the way for the dahlia's introduction to the West. Oh, the troubles it's seen!

Opposite: *Dahlia* 'Kidd's Climax'

THE AZTEC WAR FLOWER 🐝

In the sixteenth century, when Aztec gardeners showed the deep red, eight-petaled flower, *Dahlia coccinea*, to Spanish botanist and physician Francisco Hernandez, they recounted the centuries-old myth surrounding the plant. The Earth-goddess Serpent Woman was ordered by the sky gods to impale a flower of *Dahlia coccinea* — forebear of the dahlias we know today — on the sharp point of a maguey leaf and to hold both to her heart all night. Next morning she gave birth to Uitzilopochtli, the war god, fully grown, fully armed, and with a thirst for blood from the flower's "eight blood-red rays." It became a tradition that, before cutting the hearts out of their victims, Aztecs surrounded the sacrificial stone with maguey leaves and dahlia flowers as an offering to Serpent Woman and the war god.

Another, more practical, species shown to Hernandez was *Dahlia imperialis*, called Hollow Pipe, a tree dahlia which grew to heights of thirty feet or more. Aztecs demonstrated how they used the hollow stems of these dahlias to construct a viaduct-like system that carried water over long distances.

Aztecs cultivated plants, which clearly indicated that they were familiar with hybridizing. Hernandez learned that Nahuatl, the language of the Aztecs, provided words to classify plants according to their habitat, method of growth, shape, form, and fragrance, demonstrating advanced botanical knowledge. A double-flowering variety of dahlia — *Dahlia variabilis* (also called *Dahlia pinnata*) — with different color combinations had been developed. It is the original of the Show, Fancy, and Pompon types of dahlia grown today. The species name for dahlia in Nahuatl is *cocoxochitl*. Other Nahuatl words familiar to us that aren't such tongue twisters are avocado, tomato, and chocolate, a favorite beverage of the Aztec hoi polloi. Hundreds of plants were grown and used for medicine. An Aztec herbalist cites that a poultice including leaves of *acocohxihuitl*, a species of dahlia, was part of a cure for epilepsy. The patient was also instructed to eat "the brain of a fox and a weasel, cooked."

Ingenious Aztecs created gardens from swamps by scooping up fertile mud to form islands known as *chinampas*. Older natives nostalgically described Emperor Montezuma's extensive gardens as having been "refreshing, with many trees and

COCOXOCHITL.

Above: This double variety of dahlia was drawn by Spaniard Fernando Hernandez in 1570, showing that the ancient Aztecs were skilled hybridizers of the single native *Dahlia coccinea* (seen opposite in a nineteenth-century illustration).

Today Aztecs still tend island gardens in Xochimilco near Mexico City. Here a boatman propels white dahlias — or *cocoxochitl* as he would call them in the language of his ancestors — to market. Both boats also carry poinsettias, another Mexican flower.

Opposite: An early frost bejewels this late-blooming dahlia.

sweet-scented flowers." The Aztec gardens were destroyed by the Spanish when they drained lakes and canals in order to build Mexico City. Hernandez was told that Montezuma's final wish, granted by conqueror Hernando Cortes, was to see his gardens one last time before being executed.

One expanse of Aztec wetland was spared by the Spaniards — today the Floating Gardens of Xochimilco still thrive on ancient man-made islands, regularly renewed with fresh, fertile mud dredged from the shallow waters in which they sit. Brightly colored punts transport Mexican families and foreign tourists, gondola-style, through a maze of canals. Local flower vendors paddle to and fro, boats crammed with blossoms, chattering in Nahuatl. Their language and indigenous features are obvious survivors of their Aztec heritage. Here, on the outskirts of Mexico City, dahlias continue to bloom as they have for centuries.

Francisco Hernandez never succeeded in successfully importing the dahlia to Spain. It seems appropriate to the dahlia's unfortunate story that its eventual introduction into polite European society was a result of the second of the seven deadly sins, envy.

COLOR TO DYE FOR 🦋

The coveted object was not the dahlia plant, still unknown to Western gardeners, but another native of Mexico. As the eighteenth century drew to a close, the French minister to Mexico grew fiercely envious of the ruling Spanish for their monopoly on the Mexican carmine grana insect, the dried female bodies of which are used to make an intense red dye known as cochineal. French yarn-makers, famous throughout Europe for their intricate tapestries and patterned fabrics, longed for cochineal dye to enhance their threads. By banning exportation of carmine grana insects from Mexico, the Spaniards limited production of cochineal dye, thus keeping its price inflated.

If only somebody could be persuaded to smuggle carmine grana insects to France, reasoned the French minister, cochineal dye would flow like wine. Fate led him to Nicholas Thierry de Menonville, an impecunious French botanist, languishing in

Empress Josephine's garden at Malmaison was one of only two in France in which dahlias grew. But not long after her disastrous marriage to Napoleon broke down in 1809, some of her dahlias were stolen. In a characteristic fit of pique she ordered the rest destroyed — if her dahlias weren't exclusive, she wanted no part of them.

Mexico. Monsieur de Menonville jumped at the chance to make an easy franc. He soon found some Mexicans corrupt enough to deliver a large consignment of carmine grana to his ship. Monsieur de Menonville was pleased to see that mounds of brown plant tubers, somewhat like potatoes in appearance, had been placed along with the bugs for fodder during their voyage. The Mexicans handsomely rewarded, a satisfied de Menonville set sail for France with his cargo of entomological contraband.

It wasn't long, however, before de Menonville's smugness turned to panic. The Mexican insects began to drop like flies. By the time the ship reached France, insect corpses lay inches deep around fat lusty roots — dahlia tubers! — that sat uneaten, not an insect bite taken. One can only imagine that the wily Mexicans, knowing full well that carmine grana insects existed only on cactus, purposely supplied dahlia tubers instead, so that the cactus-starved bugs would perish and thus the source of valuable cochineal dye would remain Mexico's exclusive property.

In France, the dahlias languished dockside — accomplices to a Montezuma's revenge of sorts — until somehow some tubers found their way into the hands of Empress Josephine.

THE EMPRESS'S GREEN THUMB 🕮

It might be difficult to imagine soil-encrusted dahlia tubers in the undoubtedly fair hands of the noblewoman whose beauty bedazzled Napoleon Bonaparte, emperor of France, but Josephine, the eldest daughter of an impoverished aristocrat, was an avid gardener. A childhood spent in lush Martinique had given her a lifelong love of plants and flowers. In 1809, when her disastrous marriage to Bonaparte was annulled, a distraught Josephine fled the court of Napoleon for Malmaison, her country residence. At the aptly named Malmaison — the house, although exorcised of a ninth-century ghost, retained a grim and desolate atmosphere — Josephine took solace from her extensive gardens.

Josephine's gardening expertise soon paid off when her dahlias thrived and blossomed. They quickly became the object of much envy. Hers was one of only two gardens in France known to contain the Aztec flower. The gardener at the other, M. Thouin at the Musée d'Histoire Naturelle in Paris, had hoped the tubers might be

Opposite: Artist Jean Louis Victor Viger du Vigneau portrayed Empress Josephine in her garden at Malmaison during happier times, before she lost her dahlias — and her man.

Opposite and below: Two nineteenth-century representations of double varieties of dahlia.

an alternative to the potato, but their taste was found to be unpleasant. One Victorian later described dahlia tubers as having "a repulsive, nauseous, peppery taste." Dahlia blooms, however, were much admired, and the dahlia plant soon became highly sought after, and thus valuable.

It was said that a dahlia tuber, if found, could be exchanged for a substantial diamond. Josephine jealously guarded her precious dahlia collection, but a visiting Polish count, in league with a lady-in-waiting, bribed one of the gardeners to remove a hundred plants from the garden. When Josephine discovered the theft, she was so incensed that she banished her lady-in-waiting, fired the gardener, and ordered all her dahlia tubers destroyed, cut up, and dug into the ground. At the idea that her exclusive hold on the dahlia had been loosened, Josephine willfully turned her priceless collection into mulch.

Later, a lonely Josephine, in her fifties and knowing that Napoleon's second wife had not been allowed to accompany him in his exile on the island of Elba, wrote to Napoleon begging permission to join him. Death spared Josephine more heartbreak. She expired in 1814 before Napoleon's reply — his final rejection — reached her at Malmaison.

Josephine's dahlias soon became commonplace. The plant was popular in Germany, where Goethe claimed the dahlia as one of his favorite blossoms. Later in the nineteenth century, French painter Henri Fantin-Latour regularly featured dahlia flowers in his still-life portraits. But nobody took up the dahlia quite like the British, who embraced the plant with all the fervor of an ardent lover.

I SAY DAHLIA AND YOU SAY GEORGIANA

The dahlia had originally been named by Abbé Cavanilles of the Royal Gardens at Madrid in honor of the Swedish botanist Andreas Dahl. But in Russia the dahlia was named *Georgine* after renowned Russian botanist Georgi. There was an unsuccessful attempt in Western Europe to change the dahlia nomenclature to *Georgiana* to avoid potential confusion with the *Dalea*, a large tribe of American leguminous plants named after English botanist Dr. Samuel Dale. This potential conflict arose because the dahlia plant, as Sir Joseph Paxton haughtily described in his 1838 book, *A Practical Treatise on the Cultivation of the Dahlia*, "is frequently, but vulgarly, pronounced dáylia."

GOD SAVE OUR DAHLIA 🐝

Dahlia seeds had been sent in 1798 to Kew Gardens by the Marchioness of Bute, whose husband was British ambassador in Madrid. But the plants were misunderstood and died after a few years. *Curtis's Botanical Magazine* reproduced illustrations of *Dahlia coccinea* blooms with the caption: "June 1803, at Mr. Fraser's, of Sloane Square, who has the credit of introducing this ornamental plant among us from France." Whether Mr. Fraser's plants were also short-lived isn't known, but the successful introduction of the dahlia to England is attributed to the colorful Lady Holland — she and her elderly first husband were divorced when she ran away to Spain with the dashing Lord Holland. In 1804, she sent some dahlia seeds from Madrid to Lord Holland's Italian librarian, Sr. Buonaiuti, in London, who soon triumphed by producing both flowers and more seeds. Lord Holland was so enamored of his wife he later wrote the following poem:

> *The Dahlia you brought to our isle*
> *Your praises for ever shall speak;*
> *Mid gardens as sweet as your smile.*
> *And colour as bright as your cheek.*

By 1826, sixty varieties were recorded. A huge advantage of the dahlia is that, along with the tulip, it has more capacity for variation than any other known flower. By 1841, as many as 1,200 varieties had been developed. Sir Joseph Paxton exclaimed, in his *Practical Treatise on the Cultivation of the Dahlia,* written in 1838, "What abundant cause have we for wonder and astonishment! Each succeeding year produces some fresh beauties to admire; each revolving season develops some new peculiarities of shape and colour." Such was the dahlia's potential for hybridization that Darwin is known to have pointed to the plant as an example of his well-known theory of evolution, citing the huge quantity of varieties descending from a single species.

Dahlias matched perfectly the flamboyant Victorian gardening style, which seemed curiously at odds with their uptight morality. The innovation of Victorian hothouses allowed British estate gardeners to "bed out" lavish expanses of garden filled with dahlias. It wasn't long before hardier varieties had been developed and anyone could grow a dahlia. In 1842, scarlet and yellow dahlia blossoms decorated triumphal arches of every Scottish village through which Queen Victoria drove on

Opposite: In early 1940, the year this *Self-Portrait* was painted, Frida Kahlo was divorced from her philandering husband, the famed muralist Diego Rivera. They were re-married that December. As well as including dahlias, Kahlo often echoed injurious Christian imagery in her art, such as the crown-of-thorns necklace in this painting.

Mexican artist Frida Kahlo often portrayed herself wearing dahlias. The native flower was the proud symbol of the new socialist Mexico, of which she considered herself a part. She never truly recovered from a crippling traffic accident she experienced as a young woman. Kahlo often painted her disturbing self-portraits from her bed — many of them dwell on dismemberment and death.

Miss Congeniality

Floral spirit-lifter for the city-dweller, sanguine superstar
of container gardens — geraniums make jolly good company

There's something reassuring about geraniums. They can be depended upon to bloom abundantly all summer with no more grooming than a little dead-heading now and then. In the many languages of flowers, the pelargonium — the cheery plant most of us think of when we mention geraniums — represents comfort. It's difficult to imagine European towns and North American streets without the convivial presence of brightly colored geranium flowers in pots and window boxes everywhere. Thomas Jefferson is known to have ordered geranium plants to enliven the windowsills of the White House. It's hard to believe that the geranium was once to be found almost only in sunny South Africa.

Opposite: *Pelargonium x hortorum*

A FLOWER OF GOOD HOPE 🪶

Merchant sailing ships of the Dutch East India Company, founded in 1602, made a habit of stopping at the southernmost tip of Africa for fresh drinking water on their lengthy voyages between Europe and the Spice Islands of the Far East. Sailors with a botanical bent, gone ashore towards dusk on a water-gathering mission, must have been attracted by the strong perfume of cloves that emanated from clumps of shrubby plants with green-and-brown-striped leaves. The dull, brick-colored flowers wouldn't have appeared particularly interesting, but the seeds were probably considered worth gathering for the sake of the spicy aroma that the plant exuded. Or perhaps one or two sailors took the chance of digging up a whole plant, which somehow survived the journey to Holland. It's foliage and scent would doubtless have lifted the seafarers' spirits during monotonous weeks at sea, guaranteeing the plant some tender, loving care. *Pelargonium triste*, as the species was called, soon became popular in Europe and is described in John Gerard's *Herball*, revised by Thomas Johnson in 1633. The common name given to it, Sweet Indian Stork's-bill, suggests that it was mistakenly thought to have been brought from India.

> ### A GERANIUM IS A GERANIUM IS A GERANIUM
> Three distinct but similarly named divisions form most of the sprawling geranium family, known as *Geraniaceae*. They are: the *Geranium*, known as cranesbill and native to Europe, Asia, North America, and other locales; the *Erodium*, sometimes called heronsbill and found on the Mediterranean coast; and the *Pelargonium*, commonly called geranium, most species native to South Africa but also found in Syria, Australia, New Zealand, and islands in the Indian Ocean. To add to the confusion, *Pelargonium* is named for the greek *pelargos*, or stork, giving all three plants associations with different long-billed wading birds. (Their seed pods resemble the round heads and curved beaks of the three birds.) This, combined with identical Latin and common names, causes headaches for botanists and gardeners alike.
>
> So, to clarify, when a garden purist asks for a *Geranium* at a nursery, they're talking Latin and expecting to receive the perennial cranesbill, whereas most people who request a geranium for their planter or window box in the early summer are most certainly speaking colloquial English and are actually seeking a *Pelargonium*. The few people who ask for *Erodium* or heronsbill are usually disappointed — not being much in demand, heronsbill are rarely in stock.

In March 1647, the Dutch ship *Nieuwe Haarlem* ran into a raging tempest just off the Cape of Storms, as the tip of Africa had become known. The ship sank, but some survivors were washed ashore, bedraggled and exhausted. The shipwrecked victims built a shelter, calling it the Sand Fort of the Cape of Good Hope. The new, upbeat name proved appropriate, for the castaways were eventually rescued after surviving comfortably for twelve months. Their description of the lush and fertile area they'd inhabited for a year, with no hostile natives to speak of or any other rival

Opposite: *Pelargonium glorianum*, or "Queen of Portugal's Stork's-bill," as geranium expert Robert Sweet captioned this 1820 illustration.

European settlers close at hand, inspired an attempt at colonization of the Cape of Good Hope. A Dutch expedition of ninety Calvinist settlers, under the command of Jan van Riebeeck, founded the first permanent settlement in 1652. By 1680, the colony had grown to include 289 Europeans and 191 slaves. In the same year a visiting Dutchman, Paul Hermann, professor of botany at the University of Leyden, collected geraniums that ten years later were well established at the Royal Botanic Gardens, Kew. Some twenty varieties of geranium found their way to Europe over the next ninety years, but in the early 1770s a veritable deluge of geraniums was exported from the Cape of Good Hope in just one shipment, due to the unlikely partnership of an impulsive Swede and a tireless Scot.

A TALE OF TWO BOTANISTS 🐎

The Swede, Carl Pehr Thunberg, arrived at the Cape in June 1772 a very sick man. On the voyage he'd been served pancakes made with a batter of flour and white lead. Perhaps Thunberg's truculent and confrontational personality hadn't endeared him to the ship's cook, or maybe the seasoning of poisonous powdered lead was merely an accident. Whichever, the resilient Thunberg had recovered enough by August to embark on an eight-hundred-mile exploration of the country surrounding the Cape of Good Hope. Thunberg was obviously in no hurry to continue his journey to Japan, where he'd been offered a position with the Dutch East India Company. On his return to Cape Town, Thunberg found none of the anticipated funds he'd been expecting from Holland. By the time he met a newly arrived Scot, Francis Masson, late in 1772, Thunberg was so impecunious that he'd been forced to take up his original profession as a doctor. (Although a bona fide physician, some of Thunberg's simple-minded journal entries lead one to wonder how he ever managed to qualify. He once wrote, "Water is the element that has allowed the Dutch to develop their shipping.") Masson, on the other hand, was comparatively affluent, with an expense account of £200 given to him by Joseph Banks, the plant-hunting director of Kew Gardens. It's likely the boastful Thunberg set out to impress Masson with his knowledge of the country, presenting himself as an

Pelargonium hortorum 'Sunbelt Coral'

The partnership of sober Scot Francis Masson (left) and swaggering Swede Carl Pehr Thunberg (below) resulted in a deluge of geraniums sent from South Africa. Neverthless, their relationship was fraught with differences.

invaluable guide to any plant-hunting expedition. He is sure to have bragged of his acquaintance with the great botanist Linnaeus, whom he had known in Sweden.

Their expedition took them across the veldt, which Masson describes as rich with flowers of "exquisite beauty and fragrance." They were astounded by the number of different geraniums they encountered. They collected seeds from geraniums with plain and striped leaves, with flowers of differing sizes and in different colors, and some had foliage scented with citrus or spices. Their route took them over the Blue Mountains which, although challenging, were the site for yet more fascinating varieties of geranium as well as orchids, ixias, and lilies. By this time the two men were becoming more familiar with each other, and it's obvious from Masson's writings that the modest Scot was finding the swaggering Swede irritating, to say the least. The two men's differing accounts of the same mishap while crossing a swollen river illustrates perfectly their opposing characters.

Thunberg blames the incident on his own bravery. He claims that he was always forced to take the lead over the other, timorous members of the party, and therefore had the misfortune to encounter on horseback an unexpected underwater hippopotamus hole that could have been disastrous, "if I, who have always had the good fortune to possess myself in the greatest of dangers, had not with the greatest calm and composure, guided the animal . . . and kept myself fast in the saddle."

Masson describes the same scene somewhat differently: "The Dr. imprudently took the ford without the least enquiry, when on a sudden he and his horse plunged head over ears into a pit and [he] was dragged out by his horse."

Another of Thunberg's foolish stunts put him out of action for several days. At one of their rest stops he insisted on sunbathing for far too long in blistering sunshine with only a handkerchief to maintain his modesty. The Swede was prostrated by sunburn and the expedition was delayed until he'd recovered sufficiently to continue.

Nevertheless, their plant-collecting expedition was a huge success. When their wagon rolled into Cape Town, it creaked under the weight of seeds, tubers, bulbs, and living specimens of plants such as geranium, mesembryanthemum, heath, oxalis, and lobelia. Masson is credited with the introduction of at least fifty different geraniums to England. Joseph Banks praised the success of the expedition in his

Opposite:
*Pelargonium
hortorum* 'Sassy'

68

own peculiar fashion: "His Majesty's appointment of Mr. Masson is to be accounted among the very few Royal bounties which has not been misapplied."

However, Francis Masson was never given his just reward. He continued to labor diligently and somewhat obscurely as a plant collector for Kew Gardens. In 1781, Sir Joseph Banks was made a baronet in recognition of his accomplishments at Kew, achieved in part by Masson's efforts. In 1797, Banks heartlessly dispatched Masson, a man accustomed to subtropical climates and now in his late fifties, to Canada. One of his last finds, dutifully dispatched to England, was the beautiful white spring-flowering *Trillium grandiflorum*. Francis Masson died in freezing Montreal at Christmas, in 1805, after a lifetime of hardship and discomfort spent collecting plants for Sir Joseph Banks and the king of England.

It seems unfair but not surprising that Thunberg fared considerably better. Somehow, after an undistinguished career collecting plants in Japan and Ceylon, he managed to succeed his old master Linnaeus as professor of botany at Uppsala in Sweden. He spent the last years of his life writing a number of botanical works, considered by some to be less than accurate. Thunberg is unlikely to be forgotten since several plants, the greenhouse climber, *Thunbergia*, for instance, bear his name. Masson, on the other hand, has only one plant named for him, the *Massonia*, an obscure and unremarkable lily.

Above: Sir Joseph Banks was delighted with the geraniums that Masson found; they helped establish Banks's reputation and secure his baronetcy.

Opposite: Robert Sweet's illustration of *Pelargonium grandidentatum*, or "Large-toothed Stork's-bill," as he captioned it.

THE BEDDING BROUHAHA 🏇

In the early 1800s, the geranium became a leading contributor to a gardening revolution that dramatically transformed the appearance of gardens forever. Despite thousands of new plants introduced to Europe and North America in the seventeenth and eighteenth centuries, a style of garden design became popular among the affluent and influential that gave little or no opportunity to display the new imports. The geometric beds of the traditional parterre garden had been an ideal medium for new varieties of flowering plants and bulbs. However, this garden form

AMIABLE AROMAS

A host of geraniums offer solace by virtue of scents that exude from their sharply etched foliage. These *Pelargoniums*, although small-flowering, yield a larger range of hedonistic aromas than any other genus.

The first geranium to be cultivated for its leaf fragrance was *Pelargonium odoratissimum*, which has a strong smell of apples. Today hybrids carry the scent of lemon, pine, peppermint, nutmeg, hazelnut, orange, rose, lavender, musk, almond, or cinnamon. The cultivation of geraniums for their essential oils has become big business. Tons of plants are harvested in Europe and North Africa and used to distill geranium essence. A large part of the essence is bought by pharmaceutical companies who use the constituent known as geraniol as a bactericide. Extract is also used by chefs as a flavoring and by cosmeticians to manufacture skin cream and perfume.

Savvy gardeners distribute scented geraniums in pots and planters along pathways and on steps. When they are brushed against, they exude their soothing scents, adding aromatherapy to other restorative aspects of the garden.

proved too small in scale for self-important aristocrats and successful businessmen of the late 1700s. The rich wanted their estates and gardens to be laid out in a much grander fashion, erroneously considered more natural because designs were based on fanciful, unrealistic landscape paintings of the time. The disadvantage of this style was that there was little or no space for flowers. Lawns, as the bland expanses of grass were called, became the main feature of the new garden design.

It's unclear who first ordered their head gardener to carve up monotonous lawns into circles, diamonds, and squares of soil (doubtless harking back to the old parterre garden shapes). Obviously it was a garden lover who longed for the permanent summer color afforded by geraniums and other half-hardy imports. These plants could withstand winter, either in dry storage or in moderately heated greenhouses, but flowered continuously once they were "bedded out," as the activity came to be known. Whoever innocently started the bedding trend could never have envisioned the ludicrous extremes to which the idea would be taken. The Victorian flower bed became a riot of garish color combinations. Plants were arranged to form carpet-like patterns that were the antithesis of natural. Garden purists were apoplectic. In 1871, the Prince and Princess of Wales, the future King Edward VII and Queen Alexandra, had their dead son's grave decorated with geraniums and verbenas which ranged in brilliant color from pink to scarlet. They were harshly criticized by both horticultural pooh-bahs and guardians of etiquette alike. The excesses of the Victorian flower bed gave bedding plants a bad reputation that endures today among some gardeners. But the geranium became a superstar. No park or public garden was without great swaths of brightly colored geraniums. People demanded them for their window boxes and planters. They were not only popular in Britain, many new varieties were developed in France, Germany, and Switzerland.

Fashions by their nature swing pendulum-like through history and the forced formality of Victorian garden beds eventually fell from grace. A more "natural" look again became the vogue, this time with an emphasis on herbaceous borders and rock gardens featuring hardy perennials. However, thanks to the bedding phenomenon, annuals persevere as an important component to most summer gardens.

In twentieth-century America, the geranium became the darling of the fashionable set. Author Helen Van Pelt Wilson, in her 1946 book *Geraniums Pelargoniums for Windows and Gardens,* writes:

> *An ancient plant, the geranium comes again into its own. So old it's new, this plant of ravishing color, of diverse form and scent is now realizing an exciting renascence. It is fast becoming the hobby plant of the century. Clare Potter, the well-known designer in New York, appeared for luncheon one day impeccably tailored in oxford grey but with an utterly feminine nosegay of geraniums tucked into the pocket of her bag. So charming was the arrangement made by her knowing hand that I had it painted and you can see it now, in all its bright gaiety, on the jacket of this book.*

Today the geranium is firmly entrenched as a permanent and genial member of the garden family, unaffected by the ebb and flow of fashion.

Helen Van Pelt Wilson's 1946 book celebrated geraniums like none before, or since.

Proud Iris

Iris's impressive resumé: namesake of a heavenly messenger;
symbol of Christ; lifesaver to a king; parfumier par excellence

If the elegant and haughty iris had a human visage, it would definitely be looking down its nose at any plant riffraff that dared to grow near it. Extravagant yet beautifully controlled blooms held high on straight and sturdy stalks that emerge from orderly fans of sharp-bladed leaves all give a distinct impression of graceful superiority. Plant collector Reginald Farrer summed it up when he wrote of the Japanese iris:

> *A proof of the brilliant scornfulness inherent in the iris may be found in the undeniable fact that it will not tolerate being mixed with other plants . . . . [I]t is always fatal and ridiculous to plant it in individual crowns among commoner neighbours.*

Although native to every temperate region in the Northern Hemisphere the iris is very much the opposite of ordinary.

Opposite: *Iris douglasiana*

A LOFTY APPOINTMENT 🏃

Perhaps the iris's superior air was inherited from the divine and self-assured forebear who gave the iris plant its name. The original Iris, daughter of Taumas and the ocean nymph Electra, was chosen by the goddess Hera to carry messages from Mount Olympus, residence of the gods, to mere mortals below. One of Iris's most exacting assignments was to inform the anxious Halcyone that her husband, King Ceyx, had been drowned at sea. The worried Halcyone prayed incessantly for Hera to protect her husband, unaware that his ship was already wrecked and the king long drowned. Hera, weary of being implored daily to protect the life of a dead man, ordered Iris to descend and break the sad news to Halcyone. Obediently, Iris tripped down a rainbow — her habitual "bridge" between the gods and humanity — and woke slumbering Hypnos long enough to ask him for help. Before falling back to sleep, Hypnos ordered his son Morpheus to carry a vision to Halcyone of King Ceyx's shipwreck. Thus Iris's mission was neatly accomplished while she, by employing Hypnos and Morpheus to inform Halcyone of her husband's death, cleverly avoided the messenger's curse of being abhorred as the bearer of bad news.

Accounts of the myth do not mention if Halcyone was disgruntled by Hera's inability to protect her husband. However, the goddess is said to have been so grateful to be rid of the irritation of Halcyone's daily beseeching prayers that she named a plant after Iris, with flowers that included all the colors of her rainbow bridge.

To this day some languages include the name Iris in the word for rainbow: *arcoiris* in Spanish — Iris's arch. The poets Milton, Byron, and Tennyson all used the iris to symbolize colors of the rainbow. In Milton's *Masque of Comus*, the Attendant Spirit, discarding his brightly colored clothes for a drab disguise, says,

> *But first I must put off*
> *These my sky robes spun out of Iris woof,*
> *And take the weeds and likeness of a swain*

Below: *Iris on Her Rainbow*, a fifteenth-century engraving by Johannes Kip, portrays Iris in her role as messenger of the gods.

Opposite: A nineteenth-century rendition of *Iris spuria*, described as a "late-flowering blue iris."

77

Opposite: *Iris
'Spreckles'*

As well as her duties as messenger of the gods, Iris was also responsible for leading the souls of dead women to the Elysian Fields, a Greek version of heaven. Families made a habit of planting purple irises on the graves of dearly departed females to gain favor with Iris and ensure that their womenfolk were safely delivered to that peaceful place.

AN ARTIST'S MODEL OF A FLOWER

Below: *Iris reticulata,*
which still grows in
Crete, is thought to
be the iris
surrounding a priest-
king in this mural
painted some four
thousand years ago.

The iris plant grows wild around the entire temperate Northern Hemisphere from the California coast in the west to the Japanese island of Hokkaido in the east, and from Siberia in the north to Syria in the south. It's no wonder that, with such a vast range, the iris is one of the most depicted flowers in history. On the island of Crete, irises feature prominently in a four-thousand-year-old mural that appears to be a representation of the Minoan version of the Elysian Fields. A young man, probably a priest-king, walks through a meadow of iris flowers. The plants are thought to be

those of *Iris reticulata*, which grows wild in Crete to this day. In the fifteenth century B.C.E., Egyptian King Thutmosis III ordered that the prize plants he brought back from his conquest of Asia Minor be immortalized in stone. A carving of an iris he imported can be seen today on a temple wall at Karnak. British iris expert W. R. Dykes recognized the Egyptian carving as belonging to the group *Oncocyclus Iris*, popularly named Cushion Iris.

The iris has been the favorite of countless artists. French Impressionist artist Claude Monet and Dutch painter Vincent van Gogh both used iris flowers as models. The twentieth-century American painter Georgia O'Keefe portrayed iris blooms as sensual abstractions saturated in color.

However, the best-known depiction of the iris is in the ubiquitous fleur-de-lys icon. It's believed that the fleur-de-lys was born out of an act of gratitude by a Frank king to a cluster of iris flowers. In 496 A.D., an overwhelming number of German Goths had pursued French King Clovis and his men into the confines of a bend in the River Rhine. With their backs to the swiftly moving river, the Franks

In the Hugo van der Goes painting of 1470, The Fall of Man, *an iris flower is strategically placed to maintain Eve's newfound modesty. In the language of religious symbolism of the time a purple iris represented Christ as God's emissary. Presumably van der Goes is hinting at Christ's message from God — His forgiveness of all mortal sin.*

had no means of escape. Clovis looked in desperation across the water and noticed iris flowers, most likely the water-loving *Iris pseudacorus*, growing near the center of the river. These yellow flags, as they're appropriately called, signaled to King Clovis that the water was shallower than he'd believed. He and his entourage were able to escape by successfully fording the river using clumps of yellow flags as their guides. In gratitude to the plant, the French king adopted the iris flower as his emblem, and it remained as a symbol of French royalty for centuries. So much so that, during the French Revolution, representations of the fleur-de-lys, as it had come to be known, were chipped off royal buildings appropriated by the new egalitarian state. But King Clovis's emblem persevered and the fleur-de-lys is featured in French regalia to this day.

Because of its name, the fleur-de-lys is sometimes thought to be derived from a lily. However the fleur-de-lys nomenclature almost certainly evolved from the expression "*fleur de Louis*," referring to the presence of Clovis's stylized iris on the banners of the twelfth-century French king Louis VII. The device soon became known as fleur-de-lys. Adding to the confusion is the fact that, for centuries, many flowers not of the genus *Lilium* were alluded to as lilies, the iris among them.

The iris of the ancient Greeks, like other so-called pagan symbols, was adopted by Christians to communicate a similar idea or principle within the Church's teaching. In European religious art of the fifteenth and sixteenth century, the flower named for Iris, messenger of the Greek gods, was used to represent the Christian Church's own divine messenger — Jesus Christ. Renaissance artists used various colors of iris to illustrate different aspects of God's representative on earth, His Son.

Irises were often employed by Flemish painter Hugo van der Goes. His Portinari altarpiece, painted in 1475, shows the Virgin and Child behind a vase of flowers, among which are a white and purple iris. If one were familiar with the language of religious symbolism of the time, one would know that the purple iris represents the Christ child's future duty as God's emissary, while the white alludes to the virginity of Mary, mother of Christ. In the 1470 painting, *The Fall of Man*, van der Goes features an iris plant growing prominently in the foreground. The purple iris flowers foreshadow God's forgiveness as communicated to humankind by Christ in his role as messenger.

Iris pseudacorus, thought to be the iris that saved King Clovis and which inspired the fleur-de-lys.

THE MOST MYSTERIOUS IRIS OF ALL 🏃

Of all the irises that were transplanted, transported, exported, and imported hither and yon around the world, perhaps the plant that garnered the most attention was a Japanese iris sent to Europe by a German doctor, Dr. Engelbert Kaempfer, at the end of the seventeenth century. Fearing dilution of its culture, especially from Christian influences, Japan had isolated itself from the rest of the world in the 1630s. Any artifact from this closed and mysterious archipelago was pounced on by the outside world with an insatiable hunger for the exotic. When Kaempfer's *Iris ensata* (sometimes known as *Iris kaempferii*) appeared, the mysterious plant was instantly desirable because of its unfamiliar origins. It helped that the graceful *Iris ensata*, since named Japanese Water Iris, bore turquoise-blue flowers of great beauty, even though the blooms were unscented.

It's typical of Kaempfer's fairness and lack of prejudice when he writes in the fascinating account of his sojourn in Japan:

> *There are numberless varieties of Feverfews and Lillies growing in this Country. Nor hath Nature been less kind with regard to the Narciss's, flowers de Lys, Clove-Gilli-flowers and the like. But one thing I cannot help observing, which is that these several flowers fall short of others of their kind growing in other Countries, in strength and agreeableness of smell, as they exceed them in the exquisite beauty of their colours.*

Japan's isolation policy, known as *sakoku*, allowed only restricted travel by foreigners under controlled supervision. Holland was one of a handful of countries with whom the Japanese agreed to trade. In February 1691, Kaempfer eagerly joined a mission, organized by the Dutch East India Company, that was granted entry to Japan in order to be presented at the Imperial court in Edo (now the city of Tokyo). Kaempfer, in his vivid descriptions of his travels, tells of his party being confined by the Japanese to their inn in the Imperial city. So protective were the Japanese of

Iris ensata, also known as *Iris kaempferi* after the inquisitive and open-minded doctor, Englebert Kaempfer, who smuggled it out of Japan.

A HEAVENLY PERFUME

In Egypt, Persia, and Japan, orris powder was made from the dried root of the iris and used prodigiously in the art of perfumery. Orris has an odor not of iris but of violets. Until the recent development of chemical scents, most violet-perfumed products were made from orris, it being cheaper to produce than violet extract. Orris also has the ability to strengthen the odors of other perfumed substances and has been used for centuries as a fixative in the manufacture of powders and perfumes.

Orris came to prominence in Europe during the excesses of the French court prior to the Revolution. It was used to mask the unpleasant smells of stale body odor prevalent in high society, since bathing was considered unhealthy. One story tells of an argument between Louis XIV and his mistress, Madame de Montespan, that concluded with the lady telling the king that, for all her faults, she didn't smell as badly as he.

Orris powder was employed to scent and preserve the odoriferous and often lice-infested coiffures of the French aristocracy. Orris was mixed with flour to make a stiffener, so that the hair could be molded into fanciful sculptures studded with ribbons, pearls, beads, and artificial flowers.

Large quantities of *Iris germanica var. florentina* are grown in Mexico today for their roots, which are shipped to France for use in the cosmetic industry.

---

their culture that the Dutch party were given rooms from which they had no glimpse of any building. Kaempfer could only see from "one single narrow window . . . the meridian height of the sun." However, Kaempfer possessed a gregarious character, a curious nature, and an astoundingly unbiased objectivity (although trained in the European style of medicine, he was fascinated by Eastern medical practices such as acupuncture). As a result of his outgoing and uncritical demeanor, he managed to befriend Japanese translators and officials from whom he obtained local cultural and scientific information. He was also able to procure samples of plant roots and seeds, with which he returned to Europe.

Kaempfer may have seen irises growing on roofs as he passed Japanese houses at the side of the road. The emperor decreed that only certain plants, none of them the iris, could be grown in the gardens of the general population. It's believed that Japanese women started the habit of cultivating irises on their roofs instead of their gardens as a way of circumventing the Imperial edict. However the *Iris ensata* he obtained most likely came from one of the inn gardens, or *tsubo*, to which he was allowed access. His description is featured in *Kaempfer's History of Japan*:

> The tsubo, *or garden behind the house, is also very curiously kept for travellers to divert themselves with walking therein, and beholding the fine beautiful flowers it is commonly adorn'd with.*

If Dr. Englebert Kaempfer had been caught lifting irises from the Japanese garden at the inn where he was staying, he would have been promptly deported, or worse. Japan isolated itself from the world in the 1630s, fearing dilution of its culture. When Kaempfer returned to Europe from a rare trade mission to Japan in 1691 bearing the unusual and exotic Iris ensata, *he became the hero of the botanical community.*

It's easy to imagine the inquisitive Kaempfer surreptitiously lifting a couple of the moisture-loving iris rhizomes growing at the edge of a freshwater pond in one of these lovely inn gardens:

... with alive fish kept in it and surrounded with proper plants, that is such as love a watery soil, and would lose their beauty and greenness if planted in a dry ground.

Fortunately he wasn't caught by Japanese authorities, who would probably have banished him. Any locals found helping him would have been severely punished. Kaempfer returned safely to Europe via Java and the Cape of Good Hope. He married, practiced as a doctor, and wrote extensively about his travels until he died in 1716.

JUSTIFIABLY IMMODEST 🐾

Records show that the iris has been used over the years to treat all kinds of ailments, from coughs and colds to sciatica and skin ulcers. William Bartram wrote in his *Travels, 1773-1778* of its use by the Ottasses Indians of North America:

They fast seven or eight days, during which time they eat or drink nothing but a meager gruel made of a little corn flour and water, taking at the same time, by way of medicine or physic, a strong decoction of the Iris versicolor, *which is a powerful cathartic. They hold this root in high estimation; every town cultivates a little plantation of it . . .*

Startlingly beautiful and useful too — perhaps the iris has every right to be proud. Here's the last word from plant collector Reginald Farrer, writing about *Iris susiana*, a native of Asia Minor with gray-tinged, lilac petals veined and streaked in purple-black:

They are chief mourners in their own funeral pomps, wistful and sombre and royal in an unearthly beauty of their own . . . they are the maidens that went down into hell with Persephone, and yearly in her train return to make a carpet for her feet across the limestones of the Levant.

Opposite: Clumps of irises decorate a Japanese garden painted by Ella Du Cane in 1908.

Iris susiana

Lilacs Are forever

Long-lived lilacs flower for centuries, but their
haunting scent can also be their melancholy curse

French writer Marcel Proust, a keen observer of the power of memory, claimed that he need only think of lilacs to be able to smell their scent. Their distinctive perfume makes such a strong first impression that most of us have lasting childhood memories associated with lilac flowers. The enduring effects of their scent match the plant's astonishing longevity. Twisted lilac trees survive for centuries, long after the people who planted them are dead and gone. On Mackinac Island, Michigan, the blossoms of gnarled but sturdy bushes, some of the first in North America, continue to perfume the air more than 350 years after they were planted by French Jesuit missionaries. Lilacs retain their heavenly scent to the end — when dead lilac wood is burnt, the smoke is imbued with the sweet fragrance of its blossom.

Opposite: *Syringa persica*

THE SCENT OF NOSTALGIA 🏃

There are some disadvantages to having a recognizable scent that pervades the air every spring. Many nostalgic memories triggered by the smell of lilacs can seem bittersweet — tinged with regret for the passing of happier, more hopeful times. American poet Walt Whitman used the lilac in his "Memories of President Lincoln" to symbolize the peculiar cycle of grief and optimism experienced by those who remain after a death. He concludes his description of the sombre journey of Lincoln's coffin throughout the States with:

Here, coffin that slowly passes
I give you my sprig of lilac.
(Not for you, for one alone,
Blossoms and branches green to coffins all I bring.
For fresh as the morning, thus would I chant a song for you
   O sane and sacred death.)

It's said in Germany that when lilac bushes bloom people become tired and indolent. The Scots go so far as to consider it unlucky to bring lilac flowers into the house. It was once believed in England and North America that if a girl wore lilac, she would never find a husband. In Persia, lilacs are said to represent "the abandoned," given by men to their lovers to warn of their imminent desertion.

A Greek legend, which involves a rejection of more dire consequence than the broken heart of a jilted sweetheart, supplied the inspiration for the Latin name for lilac, *Syringa*. The lascivious god Pan relentlessly pursued a beautiful young woman called Syrinx, who shunned his carnal attentions, wanting nothing to do with him. Pan is said to have possessed a handsome torso, arms, and head, but perhaps Syrinx wasn't enamored of his cloven hooves or his hairy goat's legs and ears, not to mention his horns. However, Pan refused to accept Syrinx's rejection. She was turned into a plant, the branches of which Pan carefully crafted into his trademark musical pipes. Lilac branches have hollow stems, filled with spongy pith, which would make them ideal for Pan's purpose. The unfortunate Syrinx unwillingly became Pan's constant companion, always at his lips. To this day the pipes of Pan are still known as a syrinx.

Opposite: Lilac's Latin name of *Syringa* is said to have originated with Syrinx, a young woman with whom Pan was enamored — as is obvious in this 1759 painting by Francois Boucher, titled *Pan and Syrinx*.

Lilas.

THE GYPSY LILAC ❧

It's a mark of the tenacity of the roaming lilac that, although its natural home is limited to selected valleys of Eastern Europe and a handful of mountain locations in Asia, it is now found in most countries of the Northern Hemisphere. The so-called Persian lilac, *Syringa persica*, is actually a native of Kansu, a province of northern China, south of Mongolia. It was thought to have originated in Persia, hence its name, but was actually carried by twelfth-century travelers from its mountainside home in China. *Syringa persica* grew along routes used to transport goods to and from Asia. Peach and apricot plants, silk, musk, and rhubarb were carried past roadside lilacs to Persia, and in the other direction walnuts, grapevines, and muskmelon were transported into China. Lilac bushes were probably dug up in Kansu by a resourceful merchant and sold in Persia. They soon naturalized and grew there for hundreds of years. Lilacs eventually spread to nearby Turkey, where Pierre Bélon, a French visitor to the court of Suleiman the Magnificent, the sultan of Turkey, encountered them in the mid-1550s.

Opposite: Pierre Joseph Redouté featured this illustration of "Lilas" in his book *Choix des Plus Belles Fleurs*, 1829.

One of the first descriptions of the lilac was written by naturalist Bélon. He recounted the Turks' love of flowers in general and described the lilac flowers he saw for the first time in Constantinople as being "*comme une queue de Regnard*," like the tail of a fox. The plant was later known in several languages as Foxtail. The common name, lilac, doubtless originated from the Persian *nilak*, meaning blue.

A few years after Bélon sent descriptions of lilac flowers to Western Europe, another visitor to the court of Suleiman, scholar Augier Ghislain de Busbecq, became the first to export a living plant. When he returned to his home in Vienna after a seven-year stint in Turkey as an ambassador of Emperor Ferdinand I, de Busbecq brought back at least one lilac bush. An account from the time describes his garden:

> *In the garden of the diplomat the Lilac bloomed for the first time, highly admired by the Viennese who stood around the garden at the corner of the Himmelpfortgasse and the Seilerstätte.*

In 1570, de Busbecq accompanied Archduchess Elisabeth from Vienna to Paris, where she was to marry Charles IX of France. It isn't known if de Busbecq took lilacs with him, but it seems unlikely he'd leave the much-admired bush behind; he remained in France until his death in 1592.

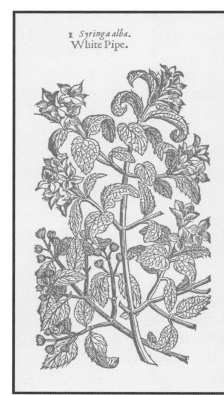

1 Syringa alba.
White Pipe.

2 Syringa cærulea.
Blew Pipe.

ONE PIPE TOO MANY

Confusion has often swirled around the difference between lilac and mock orange. At one time both mock orange and lilac were referred to as Syringa. Adding to the mix-up was the fact that lilac was called Blue (Blew) Pipe while mock orange was referred to as White Pipe. When botanist John Gerard described White Pipe in 1633 as being "too sweet, troubling and molesting the head in a very strange manner," it's obvious, judging from the accompanying woodcut, that he was describing the effects of mock orange, despite the label of *Syringa alba* above the illustration. Eventually the two became appropriately separated; mock orange was labelled *Philadelphus* (believed to be named for a fourth-century Macedonian king, Ptolemy Philadelphus), and the habit of calling either plant a pipe was lost.

Opposite: A mixture of varieties of fragrant *Syringa vulgaris.*

Nobody contributed more to the proliferation of lilacs than Victor Lemoine of Nancy, France. Towards the end of the nineteenth century, soon after the Franco-Prussian War, M. Lemoine gained an international reputation for developing many beautiful varieties of double lilacs. His eyesight failing, Lemoine relied on his wife to climb a stepladder to pollinate new lilacs, named after French countesses, princesses, and assorted nobility. Her contribution was recognized in the naming of the widely grown double white cultivar known as *Syringa* 'Mme. Lemoine.'

Canadian botanist Isabella Preston developed so many lilac hybrids she ran out of ideas for naming them. She turned to Shakespeare for inspiration and as a result the Preston lilacs, as they've become known, have names such as 'Juliet,' 'Viola,' and 'Miranda.'

A LILAC BY ANY OTHER NAME 🪰

Humans seem to have an irresistible compulsion to try to improve nature's bounty; nowhere is this more true than in the horticultural world. Hybridizers toil for years to develop a plant or flower which may be superior to a naturally evolved original. Isabella Preston of Ottawa, Canada, was a twentieth-century grande dame of hybridizers. Her lilac crosses proliferate in nursery catalogues today as a testimony to her tireless expertise.

Miss Preston, as she was always known, was employed by Canada's innovative Central Experimental Farm in 1920 and given the title of Specialist in Ornamental Horticulture. One would imagine that the biggest challenge to a hybridizer like Isabella Preston was the cross-pollination process needed to develop a new plant. Certainly Miss Preston was painstakingly accurate in transferring pollen from anther to stigma, but once this job was achieved, her most time-consuming task was to simply bag the blooms to prevent any rogue bees from interfering with the process. Then followed a year or more of waiting. Seeds developed and were planted. Doubtless Miss Preston's fingers stayed crossed until new shoots appeared. Seedlings were nurtured, buds appeared and blossomed. Eureka! But then the hard work began — what should she call her new creations? Anybody who has agonized over choosing an appropriate name for a child or pet knows the anguish of the process. During her career Isabella Preston developed several hundred botanical off-spring. Distinctive names had to be found for all of them.

Isabella Preston was born in 1881 in Lancashire, England. She emigrated to Canada when her parents died, accompanying her sister, who'd taken a job as a music teacher in Guelph, Ontario. When the Second World War drew to a close, she turned, no doubt in patriotic desperation, to allied aircraft as names for lilies she'd developed during the hostilities. 'Hurricane' and 'Spitfire' were two of the many lily plants cultivated by Miss Preston. She hit another nomenclature jackpot when she used the names of Canadian lakes as labels for each of the fifteen flowering crabapple trees she developed. In the same spirit, Miss Preston called many of her roses after Native Canadian tribes.

The Fighter Aircraft series of lilies followed on the heels of the Stenographer series. Lilies such as 'Brenda Watts,' "Edna Kean,' and 'Muriel Condie' were all

Opposite: Canadian Isabella Preston with one of the many lilacs she developed.

This nineteenth-century painting, simply titled *Lilacs*, by Ukrainian artist A. S. Yegornov, communicates the nostalgic, romantic associations that are the plant's blessing and also its curse.

named after stenographers working at the Central Experimental Farm. But a hybridizer's work isn't always appreciated. One day Miss Preston took stenographer Phyllis Cox out to see her namesake, a vivid orange-red lily. "There," said Miss Preston, "that's you." "That hideous orange thing?" replied the ungrateful Phyllis Cox. No wonder Isabella Preston turned to fictional characters for inspiration when she developed the Preston lilacs, as they've since become known. Many of her lilacs bear the name of a Shakespearean heroine, such as 'Juliet,' 'Viola,' and 'Miranda.'

Before her death in 1965, Isabella Preston won horticultural prizes and awards in England, Canada, and the United States. Sadly, hybridizing etiquette seems to dictate that one never names a flower after oneself. It wasn't until one of her late-blooming lilac hybrids was recognized as a new species that any flower bore her name. It seems fitting that American authorities named *Syringa x prestoniae* to perpetuate the memory of the inventive Isabella Preston.

THE LONESOME LILAC 🌿

Lilacs belong to the huge olive family, *Oleaceae*. Similar to abandoned olive groves that continue to grow on Mediterranean hillsides, lilac copses persist today in deserted areas the world over. They thrive and multiply in areas long forsaken by the settlers who cultivated the original shrubs. American writer Henry David Thoreau wrote:

> *Still grows the vivacious lilac a generation after the door and lintel and the sill are gone . . . little did the dusky children think that the puny slip with its two eyes only, which they stuck in the ground in the shadow of the house and daily watered, would root itself so, and outlive them . . . and tell their story faintly to the lone wanderer a half century after they had grown and died.*

A LILAC TOO SOON

To spot the horticultural anachronism in the 1966 British movie, *A Man for All Seasons*, moviegoers need to know that King Henry VIII died in 1547, at least half a century before lilacs reached England. Set in Tudor England around 1530, the film portrays the struggle of will versus conscience between King Henry VIII, played by Robert Shaw, and Sir Thomas More, played by Paul Scofield. In a scene set in Sir Thomas's Chelsea garden, the king is attempting to persuade More to sanction his divorce from Catherine of Aragon. King Henry VIII takes a break from a tirade of childish exasperation aimed at the resolute Sir Thomas. The king strides over to a blooming white lilac bush and admires its flowers. "Lilac. I have them at Hampton. Not so fine as this though," muses King Henry VIII as he plucks one of the luscious blossoms.

Robert Bolt, who wrote the original stage play and the screenplay for the film, must have been blissfully unaware that lilacs wouldn't have reached More's garden in time for the spat between Sir Thomas and the king. It's a fact that Sir Thomas More, as well as being a man of religious principle, was a fine gardener. His house in Chelsea was reputed to be surrounded by flowers and fruit trees. But the first record of lilac growing anywhere in England was in the London garden of herbalist John Gerard in 1596, more than sixty years after the scene in question.

It's an understandable mistake. Lilacs are so ubiquitous now it's difficult to imagine a time when they didn't grow everywhere. But to put the period in perspective, during King Henry VIII's reign, many people still believed the world to be flat.

Just a Pretty Face?

Discredited as a medical miracle-worker, the peony is still admired
for its beauty — now not so fleeting, thanks to human ingenuity

The spectacular beauty of the peony flower is undeniable, but what of the plant's healing powers? Bearing the same name as Paion, a Greek physician who used a concoction made from parts of the peony to staunch wounds, the plant was once thought to cure a host of ills. Although still part of the Chinese pharmacopoeia, the peony's medical reputation in Europe has been tarnished by exaggerated claims of its efficacy. But it seems that people the world over have found comfort and relief simply from the peony flower's beautiful appearance. It was so sought after that the peony was one of the first plants to be "forced" in order to extend its brief flowering period. Maybe, when it comes to the peony, a pretty face *is* just enough.

Opposite: *Paeonia lactiflora*

A MYTHICAL CLAIM TO FAME 🪰

It's thought that the Romans distributed the European peony as their empire spread west and north from the plant's native home in southern and eastern Europe. As for the world's other peony species, only indigenous people of North America would have been familiar with the sprinkling of native plants that grew along the west coast of the North American continent. And it would be more than a thousand years before Asian peonies traveled beyond the borders of their natural habitat.

Some three hundred years before the birth of Christ, the Greek philosopher and botanist Theophrastus wrote about both European peonies, *Paeonia officinalis* and *Paeonia mascula*. He would almost certainly have read Homer's epic accounts of the Trojan War. In the *Iliad* Homer mentions Paion, a physician to the gods, who was given a peony plant by Apollo's mother, Leto. From the peony, reputed to have healing powers, he made an ointment with which he staunched a serious wound inflicted on Pluto by Hercules. Paion quickly gained the admiration of the gods for his medical knowledge. Homer describes the curative effect of Paion's poultice on an injury suffered by Mars:

> *And Paion laid assuaging drugs upon the wounds and healed him . . . even as fig juice rapidly thickens white milk that is liquid before but curdleth while one stirreth it, even so swiftly healed he impetuous Mars.*

Paion's former teacher of medicine, Aesculapius, god of healing, became intensely resentful of Paion and his new-found skills. Eventually, beside himself with jealousy, Aesculapius threatened to kill his former pupil. In what seems to be a tradition of the Greek gods, Pluto gave Paion immortality by turning him into a flower, thus saving him from the murderous Aesculapius.

THE MYTH CONTINUES 🪰

There is little evidence of the efficacy of any part of the peony as a coagulant. Nevertheless the Greek myth established a solid reputation for the peony as a miraculous cure-all that endured for more than a thousand years. The peony became highly sought after during the time of Theophrastus, and its medical qualifications, legitimate or not, accompanied the plant in its travels throughout Europe.

Peony roots became so valuable that desperate measures were often taken by

Pierre Joseph Redouté featured this delicate *Paeonia flagrans* in his 1829 book, *Choix des Plus Belles Fleurs*.

Opposite: *Paeonia suffruticosa* 'Age of Gold'

An illustration of *Paeonia moutan*, tree peony, from *Curtis's Botanical Magazine.*

professional herbalists to protect their livelihood. They concocted stories of terrible dangers inherent in the harvesting of the peony root, all designed to discourage people from collecting the coveted plants themselves. Theophrastus recites a yarn warning that a person must stand windward when cutting out a peony root or the body will swell up. Another rule dictated that the plant must be dug up at night, because if a woodpecker should catch a peony gatherer at work, it would certainly peck out the person's eyes. Fantastic stories persevered and were widely believed in most of Europe until the eighteenth century.

Many of the flowers we cultivate today did double duty in medieval gardens as ingredients of medicine as well as objects of beauty. Physicians being both rare and expensive, doctoring was often undertaken by the woman of the house; her garden was her pharmacy.

Peonies were popular because they were reputed to help cure a vast array of different maladies. The most constant and often-quoted medical claim was that the peony was an effective sedative. The root was prescribed to treat what medieval physicians called "the Incubus we call the Mare," nightmares, or — more likely — insomnia. Epilepsy and convulsions were also consistently said to have been helped by the peony. A fifteenth-century English prescription for the "falling sickness," as epilepsy was known, involved writing in the patient's blood the names of the three wise men (they were associated with epilepsy due to the biblical description of them "falling down" in front of the baby Jesus). The prescription also instructed the patient to "drink for a month of the juice of peonies with beer and wine." As late as 1810, Dr. Robert John Thornton, a Scottish doctor, is quoted as saying rather dispiritedly that one of his epileptic patients "achieved a temporary advantage" from being dosed with peony root.

Eventually the peony's medical reach exceeded its grasp. A tradition had developed of hanging beads made from peony root around the necks of young babies to relieve teething problems. The necklaces were doubtless used as a teething ring, in which case any woody substance would have been as effective. An eighteenth-century British confidence trickster, trading on the peony's reputation as a cure-all and on the habit of peony beads worn around the neck, began touting a product

The peony was beloved by ruthless seventh-century Chinese Empress Wu Zhao. Her cruelty — she is believed to have eliminated rivals by having them dismembered — was well known. It's not surprising then that artists and artisans of her court featured her favorite flower in their paintings and crafts.

known as the Anodyne Necklace. These "miraculous necklaces," supposedly fashioned from peony roots, were sold for their medicinal value. An advertisement of the period boasts of their efficacy "for children breeding teeth, preventing feavers, convulsions, ruptures, chincough, rickets and such attendant distempers." Child mortality was altered not at all by the Anodyne Necklace; babies continued to fall ill, and, as science progressed by leaps and bounds, it found the peony lacking. The last vestiges of the plant's reputation in Europe as a medical panacea finally evaporated at the beginning of the nineteenth century.

The Chinese still use *Paeonia lactiflora* tubers to ease gastric disturbances, probably the effect of paeonol, benzoic acid, and asparagine found in the plant's root. However, the use of any peony plant as a medicine should be undertaken with great care — parts of the plant can be highly toxic. Perhaps it's advisable to limit the use of peonies to an appreciation of their beautiful flowers as balm for the soul. English poet John Keats, who was known to suffer from depression, recommended peonies as an antidote in his *Ode to Melancholy*:

> *But when the melancholy fit should fall*
> *Sudden from heaven, like a weeping cloud*
> *Then glut thy sorrow on a morning rose*
> *Or on the wealth of globed peonies*

The Chinese turn to the peony flower for solace during trying times. Although always popular in China, where tree peonies were known as the "King of Flowers," the plant appears to have been most celebrated during times of political upheaval and civil unrest.

THE KING OF FLOWERS 🦋

The Chinese Tang dynasty of the seventh century was not without its share of political intrigue, personal grudges, and violent acts. The most notorious character of the period was the first and only female to sit on the Imperial throne, Empress Wu Zhao, sometime referred to as Wu Zetian. To achieve such extraordinary status, Empress Wu is believed to have committed various heinous crimes. She used the

ANYONE FOR PEPPERED PEONY?
Although reputed to have a disagreeable flavor, peonies have been used throughout history as seasoning in food and drink. An ancient Siberian recipe for peony soup still exists. In England, around 1387, the Duke of Lancaster served roasted peony roots to Richard II at a banquet, along with "the pigges and the maribones, the thousand egges and the appelles."

Gluttony, the personification of one of the seven deadly sins in the fourteenth-century poem *Piers Plowman,* is enticed into a tavern on his way to church by the promise of "peper and piones, and a pound of garlic."

Opposite: A Chinese school portrait, in gouache on paper, of the Empress Wu Zhao (625-705), also known as Wu Zetian.

105

A tree peony, *Paeonia moutan,* by Pierre Auguste Joseph Drapiez.

death of her infant daughter (some say by Wu's own hands) to accuse a rival of the child's murder, thus discrediting her. Wu Zhao eliminated other competition by arranging for the legs and arms to be cut off her emperor husband's first wife and his concubine. Both women were then thrown into a brewing vat and left to die. Wu managed to keep order and maintain China's stability during tempestuous times. She also installed a modicum of democracy to government; whether from political savvy or genuine concern for the common people isn't known, but she became widely popular among the general population.

Her favorite flower was the tree peony. She ordered thousands of them to be planted in various Imperial locations. It was almost compulsory to feature the tree peony in any arts and crafts of the time, since only representations of her favorite flower were favored by the empress. The peony became such a status symbol that, when a renowned writer of the time, Han Yu, discovered his ne'er-do-well nephew was capable of cultivating peonies of unusual color, he forgave the young man his indiscretions.

Empress Wu was an enthusiastic patron of the arts, poetry in particular. Many poems written during her reign praised the peony flower. Maybe the poems lose something in translation, whereby lines such as "heart of the flower, sadness about to break" seem somewhat turgid by modern standards. Despite the end of Empress Wu's reign, the popularity of the tree peony continued, achieving ridiculous heights. Plants became so valuable that a contemporary poem cites a poor laborer's soulful thought that "a cluster of deep red flowers would pay the taxes on ten poor houses." By then, perhaps as a result of poetic comparisons of peony blossoms to the empress, the flower had become an accepted metaphor for female beauty.

Another Chinese ruler, eighth-century Emperor Ming Huang, appreciated the beauty of both peonies and females a little too much. An old story tells of the disastrous results of the infatuation of the emperor with a new young concubine named Yang Kuei-fei, whose love for peonies proved to be her downfall. Ming Huang became besotted with Yang Kuei-fei. He indulged her every extravagant whim, one of which was a palace garden stuffed with precious peonies. A vicious civil war broke out, in which many lives were lost. When the unrest began, the emperor's soldiers refused to defend him unless he gave them permission to execute Yang Kuei-fei, whom they blamed for much of the Imperial excesses that had so angered the general population — the peony garden being one of them. Loving life just a little more than his mistress, the emperor sadly agreed. Later Ming Huang ordered poet Li Po to write some lines to immortalize his dead lover. Li Po, who was reported to have been drunk at the time, was probably unaware of the irony of his floral comparison when he gave Yang Kuei-fei the ultimate compliment:

> *She is the flowering branch of the peony,*
> *Richly laden with honey dew.*

The plant became a lasting Chinese symbol of prosperity. For centuries tree peonies were ostentatiously displayed in salons and courtyards of Chinese houses to show off their owners' affluence to passersby.

By the time the tree peony reached England at the end of the eighteenth century, the Chinese had cultivated more than three hundred varieties. But nothing beats the thrill of finding a native specimen. One begins to understand all the fuss surrounding the tree peony after one reads about the experience of discovering a wild plant in bloom on a hillside in Kansu province, beautifully expressed by the articulate plant collector Reginald Farrer:

> *Through the foaming shallows of the copse I plunged and soon was holding my breath with growing excitement as I neared my goal . . . I was setting my eyes on* Peonia Moutan . . . *that single enormous blossom, waved and crimped into the boldest grace of line of absolute pure white with featherings of deepest maroon radiating at the base of the petals from the bosse of gold fluff at the flower heart . . . the breath of them went out upon the twilight as sweet as any rose.*

Plant collector Reginald Farrer was born to a well-to-do English family in 1880. Although reputed to be pompous, he could describe a peony like nobody else.

TIPPING THE BALANCE OF NATURE

For centuries resourceful horticulturists the world over have found ways to cash in on the popularity of certain flowers by extending their blooming season. As early as

The peony was one of the first flowers to be forced into bloom out of season. For centuries nurseries and horticulturalists have used hothouses for profit and pleasure.

the seventh-century reign of Empress Wu, growers were heating interior flower beds using underground tunnels full of warm air. They wrapped flower buds in paper, slowing their blooming time in order to produce blossom on an exact date. The tradition of displaying flowers during New Year was, and still is, very strong in China. Nurseries have always demanded a high price for peonies artificially brought into flower in time for New Year celebrations.

The habit has not been without opposition. Chinese philosophers, politicians, and religious leaders have all criticized the forcing of flowers for different reasons. The burgeoning of a socialist society is no surprise in a country that has often heaped scorn on "wasteful luxury" and always held a healthy respect for frugality — the acquisition of expensive flowers out of season has been considered a form of elitism. Confucians and Buddhists viewed the practice as unnatural. In his satirical novel *Flowers in the Mirror,* eighteenth-century writer Li Ruzhen presents the argument against forced flowering.

Fairy of a Hundred Flowers, a character in the novel, is asked by a royal attendant to make all the flowers bloom at once to please the Queen Mother. Fairy of a Hundred Flowers refuses, insisting that all her flowers must follow a schedule. But Aunt Wind objects: "How do you account for the fact that the peony and the green-peach blossom may be induced to bloom in winter if given warmth and special nourishment?" Fairy of a Hundred Flowers accepts that it is possible to force flowers to bloom through artificial means, but nevertheless refuses, saying, "As you yourself must surely know, the seasons must be respected."

Early or late, the peony is certainly respected and admired throughout the world — even if it isn't the medical wonder it was once thought to be.

A FLOWER OF A COUNTRY

Whether the country was named for the plant or for Paion, physician of the gods, is unknown. But Paeonia, thought to have been settled some seven hundred years before the siege of Troy, is almost certainly the only nation ever to bear the same name as a flower. Self-governing Paeonia existed peacefully for centuries, occupying parts of present-day northern Greece, Macedonia, and western Bulgaria. The country was ruled by its own royalty and controlled by a well-established government.

Paeonia is known to have possessed an army, but the tiny country's forces weren't powerful enough to resist the mighty Persians. They overran Paeonia during the Persian wars of the fifth century B.C.E. Herodotus describes Persian King Darius taking an unfortunate shine to a native Paeonian woman. As well as noticing her beauty, he observed the woman leading a horse to water while spinning flax with her free hand. Much impressed, Darius immediately ordered that a quantity of these good-looking and industrious natives be sent to Asia as slaves.

A particularly mountainous section of Paeonia escaped the Persian invasion. Herodotus wrote about tribes living in this remote area; he described their lake dwellings built on platforms above the water, convenient to an abundant and ready source of fish. But the growth of Macedonia forced these remaining tribes north, where they were eventually defeated by Philip II. By the end of the fourth century B.C.E. the Paeonians had completely lost their national identity. Only the peony plant persevered. Long-lived peonies — an undisturbed peony root will survive for a hundred years or more — still bloom today on hills and in valleys that once constituted the ancient nation of Paeonia.

Show Time

Lurid, breathtaking, ostentatious, gorgeous, monstrous.
Broadway extravaganza or a rhododendron? Not a lot of difference

Although there are more than seven hundred rhododendron species, from ground-hugging miniatures to giants taller than the average tree, most of us know the rhododendron as a midsize, evergreen shrub generously studded with large clusters of sharply sculpted flowers, often brightly colored. Garden purists are sometimes scornful — the words "garish" and "lurid" are uttered — but even they must admit that rhododendrons never fail to attract attention. When *Rhododendron calophytum* first flowered in the early 1900s at Wakehurst Place in Britain, hardened botanists, Lord Rothschild, Lord Aberconway, and Gerald Loder, were said to have circled the bush, raising their hats to it. Others abhorred the addition of rhododendrons to the garden landscape, denouncing them as ostentatious. It's true that outside of the large scale of their mountain homes in Asia and North America rhododendrons can be overwhelming. En masse, they appear menacing; a dense copse of rhododendrons seems a likely locale for any number of heinous crimes.

Opposite: *Rhododendron* 'Markeeta's Prize'

LOVE 'EM OR HATE 'EM ❧

Since *Rhododendron hirsutum*, a native of the European Alps, was first cultivated in the English garden of John Tradescant the Younger in 1656, gardeners' opinions of rhododendrons have been divided. Azaleas must be included in the debate too, because, although botanist Carolus Linnaeus pronounced them a separate genus, azaleas are now officially considered rhododendrons.

Azaleas seem to have been accepted more readily, perhaps because the scale of most species is smaller than that of most rhododendrons. Three American azaleas had become popular in England by the middle of the eighteenth century, *Rhododendron canescens, Rhododendron nudiflorum*, and *Rhododendron viscosum*. The latter was sought after because of its gorgeously perfumed flowers. The European *Rhododendron ponticum*, on the other hand, although common in Europe and North America by the late 1700s, was shunned by some because of its poisonous properties. Greek troops, retreating from Asia Minor around 400 B.C.E., were described by historian Xenophon as having been temporarily poisoned by honey they'd stolen from local hives. Some members of the *Ericaceae* family, to which rhododendrons belong, produce nectar that contains andromedotoxin, a substance that can drastically reduce blood pressure. *Rhododendron ponticum* nectar, from which the stolen honey was made, carries the potentially fatal ingredient.

Perhaps this is one of the reasons that the rhododendron flower signified danger in the Victorian language of flowers, which employed a blossom for every imaginable situation. For example, if a young woman's illicit liaison with a forbidden sweetheart was discovered by her family, she sent her lover a rhododendron flower as a warning.

By 1800, Siberian and Russian rhododendrons had been introduced to Europe. Hybrids from various rhododendron crosses were developed, but with disappointing results — the flowers were anaemic in color. Then, around the turn of the nineteenth century, a handful of adventurous plant collectors introduced a deluge of Himalayan rhododendrons that would add color to any garden palette. The Asian species, and the hybrids developed from them, transformed large gardens and

Opposite: This *Rhododendron javanicum* was also captioned as "Java Rose-bay" when it appeared in *Paxton's Magazine of Botany* in the mid-1800s.

Rhododendron 'Pink Jeans'

estates beyond recognition. Debate raged as to whether the addition of exotic varieties of rhododendron to the sedate atmosphere of European-style gardens was a revelation or an abomination.

THREE MEN, MANY RHODODENDRONS 🏃

It's hardly surprising that the Englishman who sat next to a frozen Himalayan rhododendron long enough to thaw the surrounding soil and safely remove the plant would be labeled "the man who made rhododendrons popular." Joseph Hooker, born in 1817, was the son of Sir William Jackson Hooker, director of Britain's Kew Gardens. Joseph Hooker published several books, but the most influential was the magnificently illustrated *Rhododendrons of the Sikkim-Himalaya,* published in 1851. Having received an advance first folio of the book while traveling in India, Hooker boasted in a letter to his mother that, "all the Indian world is in love with my rhododendron book."

The riotous color spectrum possible in an Asian rhododendron is well captured in this enthusiastic description from *The Plant Hunters,* written by Musgrave, Gardner, and Musgrave:

> R.thomsonii *produces interest and colour from all parts like a good orchestra producing music. Its flowers are colossal and an unforgettable red, but it also gives pleasure with its foliage. The young leaves are frog-coloured when they replace the old, and afterwards they turn a turquoise shade. And from the time the shrub is middle-aged its bark peels to reveal a medley of mellow colours from violet to bulrush brown.*

Western gardeners had been accustomed to gradual seasonal changes in the subtle colors of native trees favored by landscape designers such

This engraving from Joseph Hooker's *Rhododendrons of the Sikkim-Himalaya* features a majestic Hooker receiving a rhododendron flower from a local.

as Lancelot "Capability" Brown. Is it any wonder these vivid new shrubs with their pyrotechnic display of flowers, foliage, and bark were considered by some to be vulgar?

The second Victorian Englishman responsible for shipping large quantities of rhododendrons from Asia — Yunnan, Szechwan, Upper Burma, and southeast Tibet — was Frank Kingdon-Ward, who, like Joseph Hooker, was the son of a botanist. Around the beginning of the twentieth century, young Frank's natural curiosity took him on a Chinese journey "from the coast to the edge of the world." As a result, he was bitten with the exploring bug and spent the rest of his life traveling. When he discovered that commercial nurseries and private patrons were willing to pay a hefty price for living plant specimens, he became a plant collector.

Enthusiasm for his new occupation is evident in his writings:

. . . the valley was alight with flowers. Rhododendrons, dwarf in stature, yet hoary with age, sprawled and writhed in every direction. The whole rock floor was hotly carpeted, and over the cliffs poured an incandescent stream of living lava!

Compared to most collectors — all of whom experience their fair share of hardship — Kingdon-Ward seems to have led a charmed life. He enjoyed vigorous good health until he died suddenly, age seventy-two, in 1903, while planning expeditions to Persia and Vietnam.

The prize for the largest number of rhododendrons exported from Asia goes to a Scot, George Forrest, who exported some 250 species during the first half of the twentieth century from mountains that straddle the borders of China, Burma, and Tibet. George Forrest began adult life as a pharmacist in a quiet Scottish town. His interest in botany started with the study of medicinal plants. Given the horror of one of his early experiences in Yunnan during the summer of 1905, it's amazing that Forrest returned to the area as often as he did.

Forrest had set up a plant-collecting base in a Chinese town called Tseku where he became embroiled in a frontier dispute between Tibet and China. Tibetans

Frank Kingdon-Ward seems to have led a charmed life as a plant collector, experiencing few of the terrible hardships endured by his colleagues.

115

A tenacious rock-climbing rhododendron was named after George Forrest. Very appropriate for a man who, despite being chased by hostile Tibetans with poisoned arrows for more than a week, returned to the Himalayas time and again to collect more than two hundred species of rhododendron.

considered Europeans to be allies of China, and thus were hostile to any whites they encountered. News reached Forrest of the slow torture and eventual murder by Tibetans of a Catholic priest at a nearby mission. Forrest and another missionary, Père Dubernard, together with Forrest's considerable staff and other priests, decided to evacuate the area. They were pursued by Tibetans who eventually overtook Forrest's party in a narrow river valley. A priest was shot with poisonous arrows and chopped to bits by double-handed swords. Père Dubernard was tortured to death. Sixty-eight of Forrest's eighty-strong group were killed. George Forrest was among those who managed to escape. There followed a harrowing chase lasting more than a week, in which Forrest discarded his boots because they made recognizable tracks. He ate next to nothing and waded for miles in an icy stream in an effort to hide from the Tibetans, but was eventually spotted and shot at with poisoned arrows that mercifully penetrated only his hat. Forrest eventually managed to outdistance his pursuers. In his description of the ordeal, he wrote:

This illustration from Joseph Hooker's *Rhododendrons of the Sikkim-Himalaya* shows *Rhododendron dalhousieae* in it's native setting.

> *At the end of eight days I had ceased to care whether I lived or died; my feet were swollen out of all shape, my hands and face torn with thorns, and my whole person caked with mud.*

When starvation drove him to approach a village, he was given dry grain that swelled in his abdomen, causing unspeakable pain. He eventually reached safety at a mission in a town protected by Chinese troops, but not without one last mishap. At the edge of a field he stepped on a sharpened bamboo stake, stuck in the ground by a farmer as a deterrent for potential pilferers of his crops. The stake pierced Forrest's foot, protruding a couple of inches above the upper surface. He tore his foot free and limped in excruciating agony all the way to the mission.

Opposite: The azalea *Rhododendron calendulaceum* growing in Great Smokey Mountain National Park in North Carolina.

The North American native *Rhododendron canadense* growing on Deer Island in Maine.

Despite this terrifying experience, Forrest subsequently spent many happy years in the Himalayas collecting seed in astonishing quantity. Rhododendron species ranged from the moss-clad titan *Rhododendron protistum var. giganteum*, whose native forty-foot spread and eighty-foot height is swathed in rose-pink flowers, to *Rhododendron repens*, whose crimson flowers grow so profusely that the tiny creeping plant, when in bloom, resembles a pool of blood. He once wrote in a letter home at the conclusion of his final collecting expedition in 1932, "I expect to have nearly . . . two mule loads of good clean seed. That is something like 300 lbs. of seed."

As the seeds were being packaged by his helpers, Forrest decided to take a break; he went snipe shooting. During the hunt he experienced chest pains and sat on a wall to rest. It's reported that, after he leapt to his feet to shoot a snipe, drumming the air as it flew above his head, George Forrest fell to the ground — dead — alongside the snipe.

The Scottish Rock Garden Club announced: "The world deplores the loss of such a man, but Scotland mourns a son." To commemorate his superhuman efforts *Rhododendron repens* was soon renamed *Rhododendron forrestii*. It seems appropriate that *R. forrestii* deftly climbs impossibly perpendicular mountain cliffs using ivy-like roots along the length of its stems.

A TRANSATLANTIC EXCHANGE

The cultivated rhododendron craze hit America as a result of a huge display of British hybrids at the 1876 Centennial Exposition in Philadelphia. Plants with such aristocratic names as 'Princess of Wales,' 'Duchess of Bedford,' and 'Countess of Cadogan' wowed American gardeners. Ironically, American native rhododendrons had been used to produce many of the hybrids on show.

There was little hesitation on the part of American gardeners, already familiar with their own native species,

When showy Asian rhododendrons were introduced at Stourhead in Wiltshire they were criticized for their "foreign" garishness. This seems an odd complaint for an addition to a garden originally inspired by non-English elements. The garden was modelled on romantic classical landscapes painted by French artist Claude Lorraine.

to embrace any and all rhododendrons. In the mountainous back country of the South, wild rhododendrons were called Deertongue and Bigleaf. Some thickets were so dense and impenetrable that they were referred to as "hell" by locals. In his book, *A Natural History of Trees*, Donald Culross Peattie reveals why:

> *Tradition has it that Rhododendron hides the moonshiner and his still . . . too high to see over, yet low enough to form an impenetrable twiggy thicket of crooked stems . . . . Nothing is easier than to get lost in the Rhododendron thickets, especially where the terrain is steep.*

Some native species were cultivated. Writer Henry David Thoreau described a significant rhododendron event in his *Journals*:

> *The date of the introduction of the* Rhododendron maximum *into Concord is worth preserving. May, 1853. They were small plants one to four feet high, some with large flower buds, twenty-five cents apiece, I noticed the next day one or more in every front yard on each side of the street, and the inhabitants out watering. Said to be the most splendid native flower in Massachusetts . . . I hear today that one in town has blossomed.*

HENRY HOARE'S BLURRED VISION 🕊

One wonders what Henry Hoare II, who is responsible for one of the most beautiful eighteenth-century English gardens, would have thought when rhododendrons were introduced there soon after his death. Henry Hoare's garden at Stourhead in Wiltshire, England, was partly inspired by the landscapes he saw in Italy on a grand tour of Europe he undertook in the mid-1700s. A landowner and a director of Hoare's Bank, Henry Hoare II was among the wealthiest English businessmen of the century. After his wife died, he devoted his energies to building a garden modeled on classical landscapes depicted in paintings he'd seen by Claude Lorraine. Hoare completed his garden at Stourhead in 1780. It was a prime example of the eighteenth-century English ideal, incorporating Gothic elements — a stone cross moved from Bristol for example — with pagan Italian references such as the classical Temple of Apollo, all in a setting of water, trees, and grass.

Hoare's vision did not run to rhododendrons, but they are now one of the main reasons people flock to Stourhead. The first, *Rhododendron ponticum*, was added by

Opposite: Henry Hoare's vision of his garden at Stourhead in Wiltshire included subtle greens and the gentle tones of stone architecture like the Temple of Apollo shown in this photograph. Colorful Asian rhododendrons were added after Hoare's death — ironically they've become one of the main attractions at Stourhead.

his grandson, Sir Richard Colt Hoare, in the late 1700s. Subsequent family members introduced other species of rhododendrons. In 1946 the house and gardens were taken over by the National Trust, an organization that preserves and cares for various historic sites in the United Kingdom. Andy Mills, acting head gardener at Stourhead, said that every effort was made to preserve the rhododendron collection. He went on to explain that, if a rhododendron was threatening to obscure an important part of the history of the gardens, it was pruned or removed.

There's no doubt that the Stourhead rhododendrons have diluted the garden's classical image. Kenneth Woodbridge, in his book *Landscape and Antiquity: Aspects*

Author Daphne du Maurier employed rhododendrons to suggest the powerful reach from the grave of the evil Rebecca, who was luridly featured in the poster for the film version of the novel.

RHODODENDRON AS METAPHOR

There are few first lines of a novel as well known as: *"Last night I dreamt I went to Manderley again."* Written by Daphne du Maurier to open her 1938 bestseller, *Rebecca*, the words were uttered by Joan Fontaine at the beginning of the blockbuster movie based on the novel.

By the time *Rebecca* was written, Asian-derived rhododendrons were firmly established in the English landscape, particularly in large gardens and on country estates, such as Daphne du Maurier's fictional Manderley. In the collective psyche of the population, rhododendron flowers represented luxurious and exotic beauty. But there's little doubt they also carried ominous overtones, either because of their association with danger, from the Victorian language of flowers, or simply by the impenetrable and oppressive nature of mature rhododendron trees.

Rebecca is written in the voice of the young second wife of a wealthy widower, Maxim de Winter. Early in the novel she arrives at Manderley for the first time after a whirlwind romance and marriage in Monte Carlo. She is only too conscious of the disparity in backgrounds between her and her new husband. Prior to marriage, she was the paid companion of Mrs. Van Hopper, a rich American snob. Suddenly she must assume the responsibilities and social standing of lady of Manderley, a prestigious English manor. And then there's the specter of Maxim's first wife, Rebecca, who, although dead, holds a mysterious and malevolent grip on both Maxim and Manderley.

Near the beginning of the book she describes her introduction to Manderley, driving with Maxim through the extensive grounds, down the seemingly endless driveway that leads to the house:

of English Culture at Stourhead 1718 to 1838, claims rhododendrons have also blurred Henry Hoare's original intention to evoke the numinous. But an argument could be made that any garden, natural or man-made, with or without rhododendrons, usually succeeds in achieving some kind of spiritual elevation in those who experience it.

Fossils from the Miocene Age prove that rhododendrons have been growing on Earth for an incredible twenty million years. Love 'em or hate 'em, they're here to stay.

The length of it began to nag at my nerves; it must be this turn, I thought, or round that further bend; but as I leant forward in my seat I was for ever disappointed, there was no house, no field, no broad and friendly garden, nothing but the silence and deep woods.

Suddenly I saw a clearing in the dark drive ahead, and a patch of sky, and in a moment the dark trees had thinned, the nameless shrubs had disappeared, and on either side of us was a wall of colour, blood red, reaching far above our heads. We were amongst the rhododendrons. There was something bewildering, even shocking, about the suddenness of their discovery. The woods had not prepared me for them. They startled me with crimson faces, massed one upon the other in incredible profusion, showing no leaf, no twig, nothing but the slaughterous red, luscious and fantastic, unlike any rhododendron plant I had seen before.

I glanced at Maxim. He was smiling, "Like them?" he said.

I told him "Yes," a little breathlessly, uncertain whether I was speaking the truth or not, for to me a rhododendron was a homely, domestic thing, strictly conventional, mauve or pink in colour, standing one beside the other in a neat round bed. And these were monsters, rearing to the sky, massed like a battalion, too beautiful I thought, too powerful . . .

A nineteenth-century rendition of *Rhododendron arboreum var. roseum.*

Daphne du Maurier's inspired description of Manderley's rhododendrons as seen through the eyes of the mild-mannered second Mrs. de Winter leaves no doubt in readers' minds that the newcomer is in for one hell of a rough time in filling Rebecca's shoes as the new lady of the manor.

The Golden Touch

The darling of the Ottoman Empire; loved, loathed, then cherished in the Netherlands; tulips usually mean big business for somebody

Tulips appear innocent — even the armies of them that march across municipal parks and the gardens of government buildings look harmless enough. Yet the tulip's shape-shifting abilities, unpredictable as a mythical coyote, have had the power to incite the most level-headed to outrageous acts of passion and greed. A dizzying number of tulip varieties has stumped the most conscientious of botanical taxonomists. Their beauty has been celebrated at parties that would impress any event planner anywhere. Tulips can always be relied on to astonish and amaze.

Opposite: *Tulipa* 'Zomerschon'

A CHAMELEON OF A FLOWER ❧

Tulips are reputed to be native only to parts of central Asia. Yet claims of indigenous tulips in unlikely locales such as Wales or Ceylon are almost to be believed, because the flower never ceases to surprise — a quality that has made the tulip a valuable commodity.

Tulips growing wild outside the plant's natural habitat, a narrow corridor stretching from central Turkey in the west to the border of China in the east, are in fact escaped, naturalized varieties. The tulip flower decoration on a Cretan jar unearthed from the Palace of Minos indicates that wild tulips were blooming on the Mediterranean island some four thousand years ago — as they do today. But the first tulip was probably carried to Crete by an Asian adventurer with a botanical bent.

Whatever their birthplace, the intriguing thing about tulips is their tendency to change color and shape for no apparent reason. Sixteenth-century botanist John Gerard said that it was "nature seeming to play more with this floure than with any other that I do know." Anna Pavord, in her wonderful, must-read book *The Tulip*, published in 1999, described the discrepancies in tulips she found growing wild in eastern Turkey:

> *If you found two flowers that seemed the same, you would soon discover that their leaves were different. If sets of leaves seemed similar, then the flowers cocked a snook at you as they flaunted yellow feathering on their red petals, or showed that they could do without their black basal blotches altogether.*

First reports of cultivated tulips came from sixteenth-century visitors to the gardens of Turkey. In the 1550s, Augier Ghislain de Busbecq, ambassador to the court of Suleiman the Magnificent, sultan of Turkey, wrote of his journey from Adrianople to Constantinople:

> *An abundance of flowers was everywhere offered to us — Narcissus, Hyacinths, and those which the Turks call "tulipam." Scent in tulips is either wanting or very slight; they are admired for the variety and beauty of their colours. The Turks cultivate flowers with extreme zeal, and though they are careful people do not hesitate to pay a considerable sum for an exceptional flower.*

Unless he was quoting a colloquialism, de Busbecq seems to have been mistaken about the translation of *tulipam* — the Turkish word for tulip is *lalé*.

Opposite: This illustration of *Tulipa praecox* is from G. Willis's 1850s book, *The Ornamental Flower Garden and Shrubbery*. The book title boasted that it contained "coloured figures and descriptions of the most beautiful and curious flowering plants and shrubs cultivated in Great Britain."

Perhaps de Busbecq heard his interpreter compare the tulip flower to a turban, because of its shape, like an inverted tulip flower. Turks were also in the habit of tucking a tulip into their turbans, which may have contributed to any misinterpretation. Tulips were so favored throughout the Turkish Ottoman Empire that the flower was depicted in every area of arts and crafts, from fabric to tiles. The tulip was also cultivated and valued in Iran and India. According to Persian legend, the tulip first grew out of drops of blood shed by a lover. The red tulip has been the symbol of constant love in many cultures ever since.

And, like many flower fanciers before and since, Turkish florists loved the tulip for its chameleon-like ability to produce different shades of bloom and for its shape-altering qualities from one year to the next. There was no shortage of new colors and varying petal forms, the most unusual of which commanded the highest of prices.

THE ECONOMIC MAGIC SHOW TAKES SHAPE ⚘

In the late 1550s, de Busbecq sent tulips from Turkey to his botanist friend, Charles de l'Ecluse, known as Clusius, who was employed by the Imperial Gardens in Vienna. There are some records of tulips growing in Europe before this event, but Clusius's tulip collection is thought to be the original source of most of today's bulbs. However, if Clusius had held sway, his tulips would never have shifted from his garden in Leiden. When he moved in 1593 to take up a new position at Leiden

Tulipa acuminata has the elongated petal shape favored by Turkish tulip-fanciers.

University, there was only one other garden in the city where tulips grew. Clusius became extremely possessive of the collection he'd brought with him from Vienna via Frankfurt, where he'd briefly lived. He refused to sell one of his tulip bulbs at any cost. As a result, a plot was hatched and implemented that robbed Clusius's garden of many of his precious bulbs. The theft is said to have dampened the disappointed botanist's enthusiasm for tulips. The thieves soon harvested seed and it wasn't long until tulips were available in Germany, Belgium, and Holland to those willing to pay the price.

For a time, after its arrival in England, the tulip was even more sought after than the beloved rose. Herbalist John Parkinson, in his 1629 book *Paradisi in Sole Paradisus Terrestris*, admitted that many tulips had

Tulips were so popular throughout the Turkish Ottoman Empire that the flower was depicted in every area of arts and crafts. A vase of tulips adorns this earthenware Isnik tile made during the seventeenth century.

overwhelmed him with their tendency to annually reinvent themselves. Consequently, he considered it impossible to describe every variety of tulip growing in England at the time. (Parkinson was a horticultural punster; the title of his book translates as "Park-in-Sun's Park on Earth.") Even during the tumultuous years of the English civil war, one of Oliver Cromwell's officers, General John Lambert, found the time to grow tulips. He was immortalized in a satirical pack of playing cards published during the time of the Commonwealth. His portrait appears on the eight of hearts, holding a tulip in his right hand. The caption reads, "Lambert Kt. of ye Golden Tulip."

In France, however, gardening had been overshadowed by religious wars; it wasn't until 1608 that there was any record of a flowering French tulip. Nevertheless, the tulip soon worked its economic magic and began to command incredible prices. A French tulip admirer exchanged his brewery, valued at 30,000 francs, for a bulb he appropriately named "*Tulipa brasserie*" to mark the event.

Passion for tulips was heating up everywhere. In Flanders, the renowned artist Rubens painted a tender portrait of his wife, Helena Fourment, in her recently acquired tulip garden. But the craze for tulips was nowhere as feverish as in Holland.

Above: *Tulipa clusiana var. chrysantha*

Opposite: This tulip illustration is one of many commissioned by Christoph Jacob Trew, a seventeenth-century German botanist and doctor, for one of the many plant volumes that he produced.

THE RIGHT PLACE AT THE RIGHT TIME 🪴

Somebody somewhere is always prepared to pay the price for a rare natural object, whether animal, vegetable, or mineral. Nowhere has this been more true than among gardeners. Everybody bitten by the gardening bug has at some time or another lusted after a plant or shrub simply because it was new and unusual to us. Most of us have succumbed, fooling ourselves that the plant's intrinsic qualities justify the cost, but aware in our heart of hearts that we're paying a premium to grow something in our garden that the neighbors don't yet have. The tulip exemplifies the insanity that can ensue when people are prepared to pay high prices for flowers they believe to be unique.

Seventeenth-century Holland's *Tulpenwoede*, literally translated as "tulip fury,"

131

but known in English as tulipomania, is well documented. In the early 1600s, prices for tulips began to rise so quickly that Dutch speculators, with no intention of growing the tulip bulbs they bought, paid ridiculously high prices in the hope that they could immediately resell the bulbs for a handsome profit.

But what started the madness? How could it grow to such crazy dimensions in a country with a reputation for such sober citizens? It's true that Holland, Amsterdam in particular, was ripe for such a phenomenon. Western European ports had begun to take prominence over Mediterranean cities such as Genoa due to the increase in trade with North America. This, coupled with the destruction of the Flemish port of Antwerp by Spanish soldiers in 1585, made Amsterdam's harbor the busiest in Europe. The city became one of the largest trading centers in the world. Standards of living had risen; unemployment was low, and tradespeople were well paid. Many even earned what we now call "disposable income." Amsterdam boasted a stock exchange; the practice of buying and selling commodities for potential profit without ever taking possession was not unknown. Also, a long tradition of horticulture existed. And Holland's expert gardeners had acres of fertile soil at their disposal.

Holland supplied ideal conditions, but for speculation to commence a commodity must exist. The tulip, with its random eccentricities and bulbs that were easily exchanged, was in the right place at the right time.

The economic boom in seventeenth-century Holland meant that many enthusiastic Dutch gardeners could afford to satisfy their desire for rare bulbs. And when tulipomania began, tulips were a rare item; in Europe they existed in small enough numbers to be considered exclusive. At first the trade in tulips was between those who grew them, from one amateur gardener to another, but it wasn't long before the tulip became an object for financial speculation. In the book *Tulipomania*, by Wilfred Blunt, a 1623 account of the sale of a tulip, *Tulipa* 'Semper Augustus,' is described:

This illustration, captioned by Christoph Jacob Trew in the eighteenth century as "Parquit Monstre," is doubtless an early version of today's parrot tulips.

Opposite: *Tulipa bakeri* 'Lilac Wonder'

132

An illustration in De Materia Medica *by Dioscorides shows tulip-fancier Sultan Ahmed III, whose official tulip grower, Sheik Mohammed Lalizare, is reputed to have cultivated more than a thousand varieties. Tulip parties in spring-time Turkey were enlivened by the soprano voices of eunuch gardeners, accompanied by the song of flocks of caged birds.*

TURKISH TULIPOMANIA

Almost a hundred years after Dutch tulipomania crashed and burned, a similar event occurred in Turkey, but this time the brouhaha was less about financial gain and more concerned with aesthetics. When prices ran dangerously high, the ruler at the time, Sultan Ahmed III, stepped in and ordered the mayor of Constantinople to control the cost of bulbs. This allowed the passion for tulips to become a celebration of the flower simply for its beauty.

It's obvious from contemporary representations of the tulip that Turkish tastes ran to flowers with more elongated petals than the blunt, cup-shaped blooms favored in Europe. As is often true, it was a ruler who made a particular flower fashionable. In this case it was Ahmed III; his royal flower beds were said to contain half a million tulip bulbs. Other prominent citizens followed his example and a passion for tulips became widespread. In his book, *Tulipomania*, Wilfred Blunt quotes Sheik Mohammed Lalizare, who was known as the "Tulip Chief," waxing as lyrical as any love poem in praise of his favorite flower:

She has the color of violet, and the curved form of the new moon . . . . Her shape is like the almond, needle-like, and ornamented with pleasant rays. Her inner petals are like a well, as they should be; her outer petals a little open, this too as it should be. The white ornamented petals are absolutely perfect. She is the chosen of the chosen.

Springtime among the privileged classes of Turkey was a whirl of parties, all designed to show off various tulip collections. At one nighttime event, a thousand blooming tulips were illuminated by colored lamps mounted on the backs of tortoises that crawled among the plants. Mirrors placed strategically in the flower beds gave the illusion of endless waves of tulip flowers.

. . . one has been sold for thousands of florins; yet the seller himself was sold . . . for when the bulb was lifted, he noticed two lumps on it which the following year would become two offsets [young bulbs] and so he was cheated of two thousand florins. These offsets are the interest while the capital remains.

As prices and profits climbed, it wasn't long until others wanted in on the action. Stories abound of fortunes made overnight. In exchange for one *Tulipa* 'Viceroy' bulb, its owner received 2 loads of wheat, 4 loads of rye, 4 fat oxen, 8 fat pigs, 12 fat sheep, 2 hogshead of wine, 4 barrels of beer, 2 barrels of butter, 1,000 lbs of cheese, a bed, a suit of clothes, and a silver beaker. Soon ordinary citizens were going to dangerous lengths, properties were mortgaged and possessions sold, to raise money to buy tulips.

As the madness escalated, astronomic prices were paid on the slim chance that a bulb might produce a new color of flower or unusual-shaped petals. Most money was demanded if it was suspected that a bulb might produce a "striped"

BIG BEAUTIFUL BUSINESS

The largest flower auction in the world is held at Aalsmeer in Holland. More than nineteen million flowers change hands every day. Tulips are the second favorite, after roses — six hundred million tulips are sold at the market each year. The Aalsmeer auction house covers 999,000 square meters (more than four thousand tennis courts could fit on its premises). The prices are controlled by thirteen clocks, each associated with specific flowers. When the market opens, each clock starts with its light indicating the highest price of the day. Gradually the clocks' lights move counterclockwise, indicating dropping prices. A bidder can press a button at any given moment to buy flowers at the price indicated by the current position of a clock's light. Those who bid early may buy at too high a price, whereas those who hesitate may find all the flowers sold. A total of more than one and a half billion Euros, approaching two billion U.S. dollars, are spent by eager bidders at Aalsmeer every year.

Some of the six-hundred-million tulips that are sold each year at Aalsmeer flower market parade past eager bidders.

bloom. These variegated flowers appeared at random, a seemingly haphazard occurrence, since believed to be the result of a virus carried by aphids. People went to extraordinary lengths in a desperate attempt to produce a "striped" or "broken" bloom. Some tried to graft halves of two different bulbs together. Others soaked bulbs in pigment. What began as an extreme horticultural interest had become a fiasco, a Las Vegas-cum-Wall Street frenzy of greed.

It couldn't last. In the spring of 1637, frustrated amateur gardeners flooded the market with tulip bulbs, cost outstripped demand, and prices plummeted. Many were ruined. The government was forced to intervene to settle the huge number of claims and counterclaims between creditors and debtors.

Tulpenwoede was an aberration in a population otherwise known for level-headed good sense. In the end common sense did prevail and the outcome has meant centuries of good fortune for Holland. What's rarely acknowledged is that the event brought the tulip to people's attention worldwide and the ironic but happy by-product of the disaster is that the tulip has hardly waned in popularity as a garden flower since. The Dutch tulip industry of today is a yearly 750-million-dollar business. In spring the bulb-growing regions of Holland attract thousands of tulip-gawking sightseers who generate millions of tourist dollars.

When it comes to high finance, tulips never seem to lose their golden touch.

Following tulipomania, Dutch artist Anthony Claesz, who painted this still life, was employed to record differences between varieties of tulip as a guide to buyers.

Bibliography

Anderson, A. W. *How We Got Our Flowers.* New York: Dover Publications Inc., 1966.

Angel, Marie. *The Alphabet of Garden Flowers.* London: Pelham Books, 1987.

Arcarti, Kristyna. *The Language of Flowers: A Beginner's Guide.* London: Headway/Hodder & Stoughton, 1997.

Blunt, Wilfred. *Tulipomania.* London, Penguin Books, 1950.

Britt, Jennifer, and Leslie Keen. *Feverfew.* London: Century Paperbacks, 1987.

Coats, Peter. *Flowers in History.* London: Weidenfeld and Nicolson, 1970.

Cox, E. H. M., and Helen T. Maxwell. *Farrer's Last Journey.* London: Dulau & Co. Ltd., 1926

Crowell, Robert L. *The Lore and Legends of Flowers.* New York: 1982.

Fearnley-Whttingstall, Jane. *Peonies: The Imperial Flower.* London: Weidenfeld and Nicolson, 1999.

Festing, Sally. *Gertrude Jekyll.* London: Viking Penguin Books, 1991.

Fortune, Robert. Fascimile of ed. Murray, 1847. *Three Years' Wanderings in the Northern Provinces of China.* Mildmay, 1987.

Goode, Patrick, and Michael Lancaster. *The Oxford Companion to Gardens.* Oxford University Press, 1986.

Goody, Jack. *The Culture of Flowers.* Cambridge University Press, 1993.

Grimshaw, John, Dr. *The Gardener's Atlas.* Toronto: Firefly, 1980.

Haberland,, Detlef. Translated by Peter Hogg. *Englebert Kaempfer, 1651-1716.* London: The British Library, 1996.

Hall, A. Daniel, Sir. *The Book of the Tulip.* M. Hopkinson Ltd., 1929.

Hancock, Ken. *Feverfew, Your Headache May Be Over.* Connecticut: Keats Publishing, 1986.

Harding, Alice. *The Book of the Peony.* London: Waterstone & Co., 1985.

Healey, B. J. *The Plant Hunters.* New York: Charles Scribner's Sons, 1975.

Hollingsworth, Buckner. *Flower Chronicles.* Rutgers University Press, 1958.

Innes, Miranda, and Clay Perry. *Medieval Flowers*. London: Kyle Cathie Limited, 1997.

Kaempfer, Englebert. *Kaempfer's History of Japan*. Glasgow: James MacLehose and Sons, 1906.

King, Ronald. *The World of Kew*. London: Macmillan, 1976.

Martin, Laura C. *Garden Flower Folklore*. Connecticut: The Globe Pequot Press, 1987.

Musgrave, Toby, Chris Gardner, and Will Musgrave, eds. *The Plant Hunters*. East Grinstead: Ward Lock, 1998.

Pavord, Anna. *The Tulip*. London: Bloomsbury, 1999.

Pizzetti, Ippolito. Translated by Henry Cocker. *Flowers: A Guide for Your Garden*. New York: H.N. Abrams, 1975.

Philips, C. H. *The East India Company, 1784-1834*. Manchester University Press, 1961.

Rich, Vivian A. *Cursing the Basil and Other Folklore in the Garden*. Victoria, B.C. : Horsdal & Schubart, 1998.

Sitwell, Sacheverell. *Old-Fashioned Flowers*. London: Country Life Ltd., 1939.

Smith, Helen, and Mary Bramely. *Ottawa's Farm*. Ontario: General Store Publishing House, 1996.

Von Baeyer, Edwinna, and Pleasance Crawford, eds. *Garden Voices: Two Centuries of Canadian Garden Writing*. Toronto, Random House of Canada, 1995.

Wells, Diana. *100 Flowers and How They Got Their Names*. Algonquin Books of Chapel Hill, 1997.

Wilson, Helen Van Pelt. *Geraniums Pelarogoniums for Windows and Gardens*. New York: M. Barrows and Company, Inc., 1946.

Woodbridge, Kenneth. *Landscape and Antiquity: Aspects of English Culture at Stourhead, 1718-1838*. Oxford University Press, 1970.

Index

Entries in bold indicate a photograph or illustration

Picture Credits

FLOWER PHOTOGRAPHY: David Cavagnaro.

ARCHIVAL ILLUSTRATIONS
CHAPTER ONE: 10, Tokyo Fuji Art Museum Tokyo / Bridgeman Art Library; 11, © Asian Art & Archaeology, Inc. / Corbis / Magma; 12, Courtesy of Hunt Institute for Botanical Documentation, Carnegie Mellon University, Pittsburgh, PA, Torner Collection; 14, Courtesy of Hunt Institute for Botanical Documentation, Carnegie Mellon University, Pittsburgh, PA, Torner Collection; 15, Giraudon / Bridgeman Art Library; 18, Courtesy of Hunt Institute for Botanical Documentation, Carnegie Mellon University, Pittsburgh, PA; 20, Courtesy of Hunt Institute for Botanical Documentation, Carnegie Mellon University, Pittsburgh, PA, Torner Collection.

CHAPTER TWO: 24, Courtesy of Hunt Institute for Botanical Documentation, Carnegie Mellon University, Pittsburgh, PA, Torner Collection; 27, Courtesy of Hunt Institute for Botanical Documentation, Carnegie Mellon University, Pittsburgh, PA, Torner Collection; 29, Courtesy of Hunt Institute for Botanical Documentation, Carnegie Mellon University, Pittsburgh, PA, Torner Collection; 31, Courtesy of Hunt Institute for Botanical Documentation, Carnegie Mellon University, Pittsburgh, PA; 32, Courtesy of Hunt Institute for Botanical Documentation, Carnegie Mellon University, Pittsburgh, PA, Torner Collection; 33, Bonham's, London, U.K. / Bridgeman Art Library.

CHAPTER THREE: 39, Giraudon / Bridgeman Art Library; 42, Ashmolean Museum, Oxford, U. K. / Bridgeman Art Library; 43, Courtesy of Hunt Institute for Botanical Documentation, Carnegie Mellon University, Pittsburgh, PA, Torner Collection; 44, Courtesy of Hunt Institute for Botanical Documentation, Carnegie Mellon University, Pittsburgh, PA, Torner Collection.

CHAPTER FOUR: 50, Courtesy of Hunt Institute for Botanical Documentation, Carnegie Mellon University, Pittsburgh, PA, Torner Collection; 52, Danny Lehman / Corbis / Magma; 54, Giraudon / Bridgeman Art Library; 56, Courtesy of Hunt Institute for Botanical Documentation, Carnegie Mellon University, Pittsburgh, PA, Torner Collection; 57, Courtesy of Hunt Institute for Botanical Documentation, Carnegie Mellon University, Pittsburgh, PA, Torner Collection; 59, Courtesy of Mary-Anne Martin/Fine Art, New York.

CHAPTER FIVE: 64, Courtesy of Hunt Institute for Botanical Documentation, Carnegie Mellon University, Pittsburgh, PA, Torner Collection; 65, Both images courtesy of Hunt Institute for Botanical Documentation, Carnegie Mellon University, Pittsburgh, PA; 70, Courtesy of Hunt Institute for Botanical Documentation, Carnegie Mellon University, Pittsburgh, PA, Torner Collection; 71, Courtesy of Hunt Institute for Botanical Documentation, Carnegie Mellon University, Pittsburgh, PA.

CHAPTER SIX: 76, Courtesy of Hunt Institute for Botanical Documentation, Carnegie Mellon University, Pittsburgh, PA, Torner Collection; 77, Nezu Art Museum, Tokyo, Japan / Bridgeman Art Library; 78, Archaeological Museum of Heraklion, Crete, Greece / Bridgeman Art Library; 80, Kunsthistorisches Museum, Vienna, Austria / Bridgeman Art Library; 84, Courtesy of Hunt Institute for Botanical Documentation, Carnegie Mellon University, Pittsburgh, PA, Torner Collection; 84, Courtesy of Hunt Institute for Botanical Documentation, Carnegie Mellon University, Pittsburgh, PA, Torner Collection; 85, Courtesy of Hunt Institute for Botanical Documentation, Carnegie Mellon University, Pittsburgh, PA, Torner Collection.

CHAPTER SEVEN: 88, By kind permission of the Trustees of the National Gallery, London / Corbis / Magma; 90, Courtesy of Hunt Institute for Botanical Documentation, Carnegie Mellon University, Pittsburgh, PA, Torner Collection; 94, National Archives of Canada, PA-136942; 96, Odessa Fine Arts Museum, Ukraine / Bridgeman Art Library.

CHAPTER EIGHT: 100, Courtesy of Hunt Institute for Botanical Documentation, Carnegie Mellon University, Pittsburgh, PA, Torner Collection; 102, Courtesy of Hunt Institute for Botanical Documentation, Carnegie Mellon University, Pittsburgh, PA, Torner Collection; 104, Archives Charmet / Bridgeman Art Library; 106, Courtesy of Hunt Institute for Botanical Documentation, Carnegie Mellon University, Pittsburgh, PA, Torner Collection; 107, Courtesy of Hunt Institute for Botanical Documentation, Carnegie Mellon University, Pittsburgh, PA; 108, The Stapleton Collection / Bridgeman Art Library; 109, © Asian Art & Archaeology, Inc. / Corbis / Magma.

CHAPTER NINE: 112, Courtesy of Hunt Institute for Botanical Documentation, Carnegie Mellon University, Pittsburgh, PA, Torner Collection; 114, Courtesy of Hunt Institute for Botanical Documentation, Carnegie Mellon University, Pittsburgh, PA; 115, Courtesy of Hunt Institute for Botanical Documentation, Carnegie Mellon University, Pittsburgh, PA; 116, Courtesy of Hunt Institute for Botanical Documentation, Carnegie Mellon University, Pittsburgh, PA; 117, Courtesy of Hunt Institute for Botanical Documentation, Carnegie Mellon University, Pittsburgh, PA, Torner Collection; 120, Courtesy of The National Trust, U. K.; 123, Courtesy of Hunt Institute for Botanical Documentation, Carnegie Mellon University, Pittsburgh, PA, Torner Collection.

CHAPTER TEN: 126, Courtesy of Hunt Institute for Botanical Documentation, Carnegie Mellon University, Pittsburgh, PA, Torner Collection; 129, Ashmolean Museum, Oxford / Bridgeman Art Library; 130, Courtesy of Hunt Institute for Botanical Documentation, Carnegie Mellon University, Pittsburgh, PA, Torner Collection; 132, Courtesy of Hunt Institute for Botanical Documentation, Carnegie Mellon University, Pittsburgh, PA, Torner Collection; 134, Topkapi Palace Museum, Istanbul, Turkey / Bridgeman Art Library; 136, Courtesy of Bloemenveiling Aalsmeer; 137, Christie's Images / Bridgeman Art Library.

Every effort has been made to obtain permissions and to print credits for pictures. Any concerns should be addressed to:
PageWave Graphics Inc., 533 College Street, Toronto, ON M6G 1A8

Thanks to

Pat Kennedy at McClelland & Stewart Ltd., Toronto,
for her enthusiasm and encouragement.

Charlotte Tancin, Librarian, Hunt Institute for Botanical Documentation,
Carnegie Mellon University, Pittsburgh, who supplied such thorough and inspired
research for the text and for the botanical illustrations.

Bernice Eisenstein for her meticulous copy-editing and editorial guidance.

Anne Gibson, garden designer, for editing the botanical references, and for her sage advice.

David Cavagnaro for his beautiful photographs of flowers.

Leslie Black at Bridgeman Art Library, London, for her work above and beyond the call of duty.

Pierre Berton and Marjorie Harris for their support.

PageWavers — Kevin Cockburn, Joseph Gisini, and Daniella Zanchetta — for their
assistance and patience.

James Carley, Winston Collins, Elsa Franklin, Shelagh Hewitt, Anne Hutchison, Patty Proctor,
Barbara Sears, Carol Sherman, Andrew Souvaliotis, and Erik Tanner for their valuable contributions.

Foreign publishing rights available. Contact Marilyn Biderman, McClelland & Stewart Ltd.,
481 University Avenue, Suite 900, Toronto, Ontario, Canada M5G 2E9.
MBiderman@mcclelland.com